Pcbnew

August 24, 2017

Contents

Reference manual

Copyright

Contributors

Jean-Pierre Charras, Fabrizio Tappero.

Feedback

Please direct any bug reports, suggestions or new versions to here:

- About KiCad document: https://github.com/KiCad/kicad-doc/issues

- About KiCad software: https://bugs.launchpad.net/kicad

- About KiCad software i18n: https://github.com/KiCad/kicad-i18n/issues

Publication date and software version

2014, march 17.

Changes to original document: Color text and images were converted to grayscale.

Chapter 1

Introduction to Pcbnew

1.1 Description

Pcbnew is a powerful printed circuit board software tool available for the Linux, Microsoft Windows and Apple OS X operating systems. Pcbnew is used in association with the schematic capture program Eeschema to create printed circuit boards.

Pcbnew manages libraries of footprints. Each footprint is a drawing of the physical component including its land pattern (the layout of pads on the circuit board). The required footprints are automatically loaded during the reading of the Netlist. Any changes to footprint selection or annotation can be changed in the schematic and updated in pcbnew by regenerating the netlist and reading it in pcbnew again.

Pcbnew provides a design rules check (DRC) tool which prevents track and pad clearance issues as well as preventing nets from being connected that aren't connected in the netlist/schematic. When using the interactive router it continuously runs the design rules check and will help automatically route individual traces.

Pcbnew provides a rats nest display, a hairline connecting the pads of footprints which are connected on the schematic. These connections move dynamically as track and footprint movements are made.

Pcbnew has a simple but effective autorouter to assist in the production of the circuit board. An Export/Import in SPECCTRA dsn format allows the use of more advanced auto-routers.

Pcbnew provides options specifically provided for the production of ultra high frequency microwave circuits (such as pads of trapezoidal and complex form, automatic layout of coils on the printed circuit, etc).

1.2 Principal design features

The smallest unit in pcbnew is 1 nanometer. All dimensions are stored as integer nanometers.

Pcbnew can generate up to 32 layers of copper, 14 technical layers (silk screen, solder mask, component adhesive, solder paste and edge cuts) plus 4 auxiliary layers (drawings and comments) and manages in real time the hairline indication (rats nest) of missing tracks.

The display of the PCB elements (tracks, pads, text, drawings···) is customizable:

- In full or outline.

- With or without track clearance.

For complex circuits, the display of layers, zones, and components can be hidden in a selective way for clarity on screen. Nets of traces can be highlighted to provide high contrast as well.

Footprints can be rotated to any angle, with a resolution of 0.1 degree.

Pcbnew includes a Footprint Editor that allows editing of individual footprints that have been on a pcb or editing a footprint in a library.

The Footprint Editor provides many time saving tools such as:

- Fast pad numbering by simply dragging the mouse over pads in the order you want them numbered.

- Easy generation of rectangular and circular arrays of pads for LGA/BGA or circular footprints.

- Semi-automatic aligning of rows or columns of pads.

Footprint pads have a variety of properties that can be adjusted. The pads can be round, rectangular, oval or trapezoidal. For through-hole parts drills can be offset inside the pad and be round or a slot. Individual pads can also be rotated and have unique soldermask, net, or paste clearance. Pads can also have a solid connection or a thermal relief connection for easier manufacturing. Any combination of unique pads can be placed within a footprint.

Pcbnew easily generates all the documents necessary for production:

- Fabrication outputs:

  - Files for Photoplotters in GERBER RS274X format.
  - Files for drilling in EXCELLON format.

- Plot files in HPGL, SVG and DXF format.

- Plot and drilling maps in POSTSCRIPT format.

- Local Printout.

1.3   General remarks

Due to the degree of control necessary it is highly suggested to use a 3-button mouse with pcbnew. Many features such as panning and zooming require a 3-button mouse.

In the new release of KiCad, pcbnew has seen wide sweeping changes from developers at CERN. This includes features such as a new renderer (OpenGL and Cairo view modes), an interative push and shove router, differential and meander trace routing and tuning, a reworked Footprint Editor, and many other features. Please note that most of these new features **only** exist in the new OpenGL and Cairo view modes.

Chapter 2

Installation

2.1 Installation of the software

The installation procedure is described in the KiCad documentation.

2.2 Modifying the default configuration

A default configuration file `kicad.pro` is provided in `kicad/share/template`. This file is used as the initial configuration for all new projects.

This configuration file can be modified to change the libraries to be loaded.

To do this:

- Launch Pcbnew using kicad or directly. On Windows it is in `C:\kicad\bin\pcbnew.exe` and on Linux you can run `/usr/local/kicad/bin/kicad` or `/usr/local/kicad/bin/pcbnew` if the binaries are located in `/usr/local/kicad/bin`.

- Select Preferences - Libs and Dir.

- Edit as required.

- Save the modified configuration (Save Cfg) to `kicad/share/template/kicad.pro`.

2.3 Managing Footprint Libraries: legacy versions

You can have access to the library list initialization from the Preferences menu:

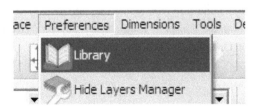

The image below shows the dialog which allows you to set the footprint library list:

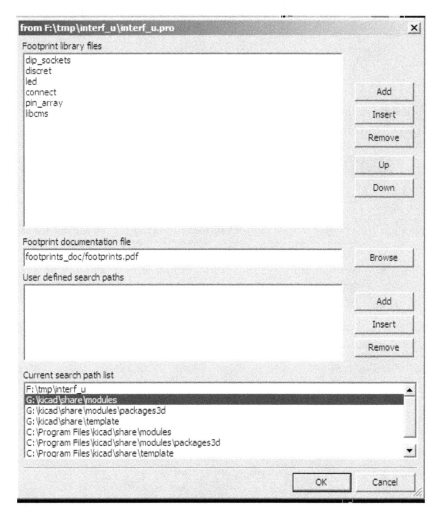

You can use this to add all the libraries that contain the footprints required for your project. You should also remove unused libraries from new projects to prevent footprint name clashes. Please note, there is an issue with the footprint library list when duplicate footprint names exist in more than one library. When this occurs, the footprint will be loaded from the first library found in the list. If this is an issue (you cannot load the footprint you want), either change the library list order using the "Up" and "Down" buttons in the dialog above or give the footprint a unique name using the footprint editor.

2.4   Managing Footprint Libraries: .pretty repositories

As of release 4.0, Pcbnew uses the new footprint library table implementation to manage footprint libraries. The information in the previous section is no longer valid. The library table manager is accessible by:

The image below shows the footprint library table editing dialog which can be opened by invoking the "Footprint Libraries Manager" entry from the "Preferences" menu.

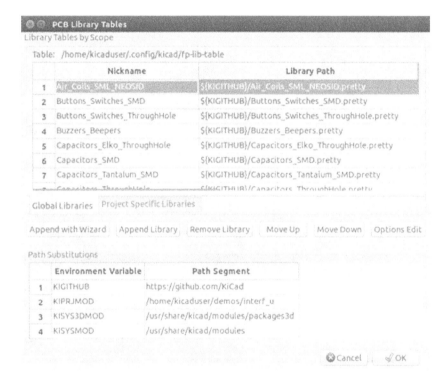

The footprint library table is used to map a footprint library of any supported library type to a library nickname. This nickname is used to look up footprints instead of the previous method which depended on library search path ordering. This allows Pcbnew to access footprints with the same name in different libraries by ensuring that the correct footprint is loaded from the appropriate library. It also allows Pcbnew to support loading libraries from different PCB editors such as Eagle and gEDA.

2.4.1 Global Footprint Library Table

The global footprint library table contains the list of libraries that are always available regardless of the currently loaded project file. The table is saved in the file `fp-lib-table` in the user's home folder. The location of this folder is dependent on the operating system.

2.4.2 Project Specific Footprint Library Table

The project specific footprint library table contains the list of libraries that are available specifically for the currently loaded project file. The project specific footprint library table can only be edited when it is loaded along with the project board file. If no project file is loaded or there is no footprint library table file in the project path, an empty table is created which can be edited and later saved along with the board file.

2.4.3 Initial Configuration

The first time CvPcb or Pcbnew is run and the global footprint table file `fp-lib-table` is not found in the user's home folder, Pcbnew will attempt to copy the default footprint table file fp_global_table stored in the system's KiCad template folder to the file `fp-lib-table` in the user's home folder. If fp_global_table cannot be found, an empty footprint library table will be created in the user's home folder. If this happens, the user can either copy fp_global_table manually or configure the table by hand. The default footprint library table includes all of the standard footprint libraries that are installed as part of KiCad.

2.4.4 Adding Table Entries

In order to use a footprint library, it must first be added to either the global table or the project specific table. The project specific table is only applicable when a board file is open. Each library entry must have a unique nickname. This does not have to be related in any way to the actual library file name or path. The colon : character cannot be used anywhere in the nickname. Each library entry must have a valid path and/or file name depending on the type of library. Paths can be defined as absolute, relative, or by environment variable substitution. The appropriate plug in type must be selected in order for the library to be properly read. Pcbnew currently supports reading KiCad legacy, KiCad Pretty, Eagle, and gEDA footprint libraries. There is also a description field to add a description of the library entry. The option field is not used at this time so adding options will have no effect when loading libraries. Please note that you cannot have duplicate library nicknames in the same table. However, you can have duplicate library nicknames in both the global and project specific footprint library table. The project specific table entry will take precedence over the global table entry when duplicated names occur. When entries are defined in the project specific table, an fp-lib-table file containing the entries will be written into the folder of the currently open netlist.

2.4.5 Environment Variable Substitution

One of the most powerful features of the footprint library table is environment variable substitution. This allows you to define custom paths to where your libraries are stored in environment variables. Environment variable substitution is supported by using the syntax `${ENV_VAR_NAME}` in the footprint library path. By default, at run time Pcbnew defines the `$KISYSMOD` environment variable. This points to where the default footprint libraries that were installed with KiCad are located. You can override `$KISYSMOD` by defining it yourself which allows you to substitute your own libraries in place of the default KiCad footprint libraries. When a board file is loaded, Pcbnew also defines the `$KPRJMOD` using the board file path. This allows you to create libraries in the project path without having to define the absolute path to the library in the project specific footprint library table.

2.4.6 Using the GitHub Plugin

The GitHub plugin is a special plugin that provides an interface for read-only access to a remote GitHub repository consisting of pretty (Pretty is name of the KiCad footprint file format) footprints and optionally provides "Copy-On-Write" (COW) support for editing footprints read from the GitHub repo and saving them locally. Therefore the "GitHub" plugin is for **read-only for accessing remote pretty footprint libraries** at https://github.com. To add a GitHub entry to the footprint library table the "Library Path" in the footprint library table entry must be set to a valid GitHub URL.

For example:

```
https://github.com/liftoff-sr/pretty_footprints
```

Typically GitHub URLs take the form:

```
https://github.com/user_name/repo_name
```

The "Plugin Type" must be set to "Github". To enable the "Copy-On-Write" feature the option `allow_pretty_wr` `iting_to_this_dir` must be added to the "Options" setting of the footprint library table entry. This option is the "Library Path" for local storage of modified copies of footprints read from the GitHub repo. The footprints saved to this path are combined with the read-only part of the GitHub repository to create the footprint library. If this option is missing, then the GitHub library is read-only. If the option is present for a GitHub library, then any writes to this hybrid library will go to the local `*.pretty` directory. Note that the github.com resident portion of this hybrid COW library is always read-only, meaning you cannot delete anything or modify any footprint in the specified GitHub repository directly. The aggregate library type remains "Github" in all further discussions, but it consists of both the local read/write portion and the remote read-only portion.

The table below shows a footprint library table entry without the option `allow_pretty_writing_to_this_dir`:

Nickname	Library Path	Plugin Type	Options	Description
github	https:// github.com/liftoff-sr/- pretty_footprints	Github		Liftoff′ s GH footprints

The table below shows a footprint library table entry with the COW option given. Note the use of the environment variable `${HOME}` as an example only. The github.pretty directory is located in `${HOME}/pretty/path`. Anytime you use the option `allow_pretty_writing_to_this_dir`, you will need to create that directory manually in advance and it must end with the extension `.pretty`.

Nickname	Library Path	Plugin Type	Options	Description
github	https:// github.com/liftoff-sr/- pretty_footprints	Github		Liftoff′ s GH footprints

Footprint loads will always give precedence to the local footprints found in the path given by the option `allow_prett y_writing_to_this_dir`. Once you have saved a footprint to the COW library's local directory by doing a footprint save in the Footprint Editor, no GitHub updates will be seen when loading a footprint with the same name as one for which you've saved locally.

Always keep a separate local `*.pretty` directory for each GitHub library, never combine them by referring to the same directory more than once. Also, do not use the same COW (`*.pretty`) directory in a footprint library table entry. This would likely create a mess. The value of the option `allow_pretty_writing_to_this_dir` will expand any environment variable using the `${}` notation to create the path in the same way as the "Library Path" setting.

What's the point of COW? It is to turbo-charge the sharing of footprints. If you periodically email your COW pretty footprint modifications to the GitHub repository maintainer, you can help update the GitHub copy. Simply email the individual `*.kicad_mod` files you find in your COW directories to the maintainer of the GitHub repository. After you've received confirmation that your changes have been committed, you can safely delete your COW file(s) and the updated footprint from the read-only part of GitHub library will flow down. Your goal should be to keep the COW file set as small as possible by contributing frequently to the shared master copies at https://github.com.

Finally, Nginx can be used as a cache to the github server to speed up the loading of footprints. It can be installed locally or on a network server. There is an example configuration in KiCad sources at pcbnew/github/nginx.conf. The most straightforward way to get this working is to overwrite the default nginx.conf with this one and `export KIGITHUB=http://my_server:54321/KiCad`, where `my_server` is the IP or domain name of the machine running nginx.

2.4.7 Usage Patterns

Footprint libraries can be defined either globally or specifically to the currently loaded project. Footprint libraries defined in the user's global table are always available and are stored in the `fp-lib-table` file in the user's home folder. Global footprint libraries can always be accessed even when there is no project net list file opened. The project specific footprint table is active only for the currently open net list file. The project specific footprint library table is saved in the file fp-lib-table in the path of the currently open board file. You are free to define libraries in either table.

There are advantages and disadvantages to each method:

- You can define all of your libraries in the global table which means they will always be available when you need them.
  - The disadvantage of this is that you may have to search through a lot of libraries to find the footprint you are looking for.
- You can define all your libraries on a project specific basis.
  - The advantage of this is that you only need to define the libraries you actually need for the project which cuts down on searching.
  - The disadvantage is that you always have to remember to add each footprint library that you need for every project.
- You can also define footprint libraries both globally and project specifically.

One usage pattern would be to define your most commonly used libraries globally and the library only required for the project in the project specific library table. There is no restriction on how you define your libraries.

Chapter 3

General operations

3.1 Toolbars and commands

In Pcbnew it is possible to execute commands using various means:

- Text-based menu at the top of the main window.

- Top toolbar menu.

- Right toolbar menu.

- Left toolbar menu.

- Mouse buttons (menu options). Specifically:

  - The right mouse button reveals a pop-up menu the content of which depends on the element under the mouse arrow.

- Keyboard (Function keys F1, F2, F3, F4, Shift, Delete, +, -, Page Up, Page Down and Space bar). The Escape key generally cancels an operation in progress.

The screenshot below illustrates some of the possible accesses to these operations:

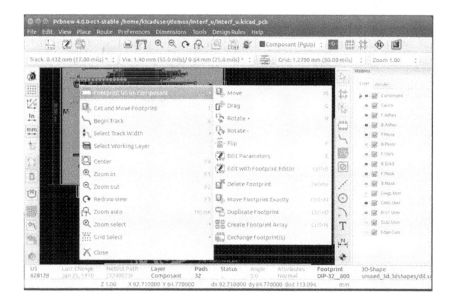

3.2 Mouse commands

3.2.1 Basic commands

- Left button

  - Single-click displays the characteristics of the footprint or text under the cursor in the lower status bar.
  - Double-click displays the editor (if the element is editable) of the element under the cursor.

- Centre button/wheel

  - Rapid zoom and some commands in layer manager.
  - Hold down the centre button and draw a rectangle to zoom to the described area. Rotation of the mouse wheel will allow you to zoom in and zoom out.

- Right button

  - Displays a pop-up menu

3.2.2 Operations on blocks

Operations to move, invert (mirror), copy, rotate and delete a block are all available via the pop-up menu. In addition, the view can zoom to the area described by the block.

The framework of the block is traced by moving the mouse while holding down the left mouse button. The operation is executed when the button is released.

By holding down one of the hotkeys Shift or Ctrl, or both keys Shift and Ctrl together, while the block is drawn the operation invert, rotate or delete is automatically selected as shown in the table below:

Action	Effect
Left mouse button held down	Trace framework to move block
Shift + Left mouse button held down	Trace framework for invert block
Ctrl + Left mouse button held down	Trace framework for rotating block 90°
Shift + Ctrl + Left mouse button held down	Trace framework to delete the block
Centre mouse button held down	Trace framework to zoom to block

When moving a block:

- Move block to new position and operate left mouse button to place the elements.

- To cancel the operation use the right mouse button and select Cancel Block from the menu (or press the Esc key).

Alternatively if no key is pressed when drawing the block use the right mouse button to display the pop-up menu and select the required operation.

For each block operation a selection window enables the action to be limited to only some elements.

3.3 Selection of grid size

During element layout the cursor moves on a grid. The grid can be turned on or off using the icon on the left toolbar.

Any of the pre-defined grid sizes, or a User Defined grid, can be chosen using the pop-up window, or the drop-down selector on the toolbar at the top of the screen. The size of the User Defined grid is set using the menu bar option Dimensions → User Grid Size.

3.4 Adjustment of the zoom level

The zoom level can be changed using any of the following methods:

- Open the pop-up window (using the right mouse button) and then select the desired zoom.

- Use the following function keys:

  - F1: Enlarge (zoom in)

  - F2: Reduce (zoom out)

  - F3: Redraw the display

  - F4: Centre view at the current cursor position

- Rotate the mouse wheel.

- Hold down the middle mouse button and draw a rectangle to zoom to the described area.

3.5   Displaying cursor coordinates

The cursor coordinates are displayed in inches or millimetres as selected using the *In* or *mm* icons on the left hand side toolbar.

Whichever unit is selected Pcbnew always works to a precision of 1/10,000 of inch.

The status bar at the bottom of the screen gives:

- The current zoom setting.

- The absolute position of the cursor.

- The relative position of the cursor. Note the relative coordinates (x,y) can be set to (0,0) at any position by pressing the space bar. The cursor position is then displayed relative to this new datum.

In addition the relative position of the cursor can be displayed using its polar co-ordinates (ray + angle). This can be turned on and off using the icon in the left hand side toolbar.

3.6   Keyboard commands - hotkeys

Many commands are accessible directly with the keyboard. Selection can be either upper or lower case. Most hot keys are shown in menus. Some hot keys that do not appear are:

- `Delete`: deletes a footprint or a track. (*Available only if the Footprint mode or the Track mode is active*)

- `V`: if the track tool is active switches working layer or place via, if a track is in progress.

- `+` and `-`: select next or previous layer.

- `?`: display the list of all hot keys.

- `Space`: reset relative coordinates.

3.7   Operation on blocks

Operations to move, invert (mirror), copy, rotate and delete a block are all available from the pop-up menu. In addition, the view can zoom to that described by the block.

The framework of the block is traced by moving the mouse while holding down the left mouse button. The operation is executed when the button is released.

By holding down one of the keys `Shift` or `Ctrl`, both `Shift` and `Ctrl` together, or `Alt`, while the block is drawn the operation invert, rotate, delete or copy is automatically selected as shown in the table below:

Action	Effect
Left mouse button held down	Move block
Shift + Left mouse button held down	Invert (mirror) block
Ctrl + Left mouse button held down	Rotate block 90°
Shift + Ctrl + Left mouse button held down	Delete the block
Alt + Left mouse button held down	Copy the block

When a block command is made, a dialog window is displayed, and items involved in this command can be chosen.

Any of the commands above can be cancelled via the same pop-up menu or by pressing the Escape key (Esc).

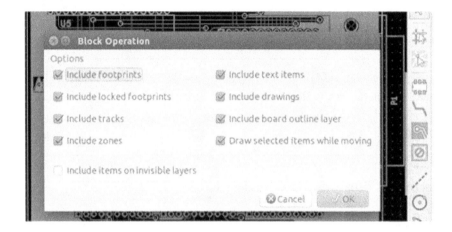

3.8   Units used in dialogs

Units used to display dimensions values are inch and mm. The desired unit can be selected by pressing the icon located

in left toolbar: **In mm**   However one can enter the unit used to define a value, when entering a new value.

Accepted units are:

1 in	1 inch
1 "	1 inch
25 th	25 thou
25 mi	25 mils, same as thou
6 mm	6 mm

The rules are:

- Spaces between the number and the unit are accepted.

- Only the first two letters are significant.

- In countries using an alternative decimal separator than the period, the period (.) can be used as well. Therefore 1,5 and 1.5 are the same in French.

3.9   Top menu bar

The top menu bar provides access to the files (loading and saving), configuration options, printing, plotting and the help files.

3.9.1   The File menu

The File menu allows the loading and saving of printed circuits files, as well as printing and plotting the circuit board. It enables the export (with the format GenCAD 1.4) of the circuit for use with automatic testers.

3.9.2   Edit menu

Allows some global edit actions:

3.9.3 View menu

Zoom functions and 3D board display.

3.9.3.1 3D Viewer

Opens the 3D Viewer. Here is a sample:

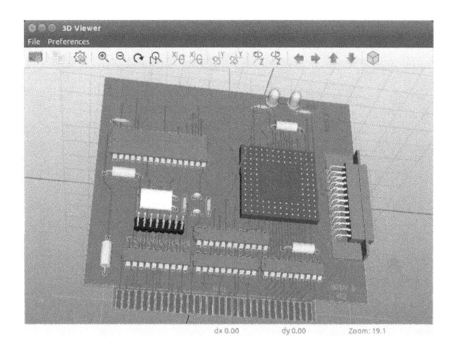

3.9.3.2 Switch canvas

Allows switching canvas.

- default
- OpenGL
- Cairo

3.9.4 Place menu

Same function as the right-hand toolbar.

3.9.5 Route menu

Routing function.

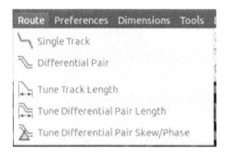

3.9.6 The Preferences menu

Allows:

- Selection of the footprint libraries.

- Hide/Show the Layers manager (colors selection for displaying layers and other elements. Also enables the display of elements to be turned on and off).

- Management of general options (units, etc.).

- The management of other display options.

- Creation, editing (and re-read) of the hot keys file.

3.9.7 Dimensions menu

An important menu. Allows adjustment of:

- User grid size.

- Size of texts and the line width for drawings.

- Dimensions and characteristic of pads.

- Setting the global values for solder mask and solder paste layers

3.9.8 Tools menu

3.9.9 The Design Rules menu

Provides access to 2 dialogs:

- Setting Design Rules (tracks and vias sizes, clerances).

- Setting Layers (number, enabled and layers names)

3.9.10 The Help menu

Provides access to the user manuals and to the version information menu (Pcbnew About).

3.10 Using icons on the top toolbar

This toolbar gives access to the principal functions of Pcbnew.

	Creation of a new printed circuit.
	Opening of an old printed circuit.
	Save printed circuit.
	Selection of the page size and modification of the file properties.
	Opens Footprint Editor to edit library or pcb footprint.
	Opens Footprint Viewer to display library or pcb footprint.
	Undo/Redo last commands (10 levels)
	Display print menu.
	Display plot menu.
	Zoom in and Zoom out (relative to the centre of screen).
	Redraw the screen
	Fit to page
	Find footprint or text.
	Netlist operations (selection, reading, testing and compiling).
	DRC (Design Rule Check): Automatic check of the tracks.
Soudure (PgDn)	Selection of the working layer.
	Selection of layer pair (for vias)
	Footprint mode: when active this enables footprint options in the pop-up window.
	Routing mode: when active this enables routing options in the pop-up window
	Direct access to the router Freerouter
	Show / Hide the Python scripting console

3.10.1 Auxiliary toolbar

Track 17.0	Selection of thickness of track already in use.
Via 65.0	Selection of a dimension of via already in use.
	Automatic track width: if enabled when creating a new track, when starting on an existing track, the width of the new track is set to the width of the existing track.
Grid 50.0	Selection of the grid size.
Zoom 128	Selection of the zoom.

3.11   Right-hand side toolbar

This toolbar gives access to the editing tool to change the PCB shown in Pcbnew.

⬫	Select the standard mouse mode.
	Highlight net selected by clicking on a track or pad.
	Display local ratsnest (Pad or Footprint).
	Add a footprint from a library.
	Placement of tracks and vias.
	Placement of zones (copper planes).
	Placement of keepout areas (on copper layers).
	Draw Lines on technical layers (i.e. not a copper layer).
	Draw Circles on technical layers (i.e. not a copper layer).
	Draw Arcs on technical layers (i.e. not a copper layer).
T	Placement of text.
	Draw Dimensions on technical layers (i.e. not the copper layer).
	Draw Alignment Marks (appearing on all layers).
	Delete element pointed to by the cursor **Note:** When Deleting, if several superimposed elements are pointed to, priority is given to the smallest (in the decreasing set of priorities tracks, text, footprint). The function "Undelete" of the upper toolbar allows the cancellation of the last item deleted.
	Offset adjust for drilling and place files.

Grid origin. (grid offset). Useful mainly for editing and placement of footprints. Can also be set in Dimensions/Grid menu.

- Placement of footprints, tracks, zones of copper, texts, etc.

- Net Highlighting.

- Creating notes, graphic elements, etc.

- Deleting elements.

3.12 Left-hand side toolbar

The left hand-side toolbar provides display and control options that affect Pcbnew's interface.

		Turns DRC (Design Rule Checking) on/off. **Caution:** when DRC is off incorrect connections can be made.
		Turn grid display on/off **Note:** a small grid may not be displayed unless zoomed in far enough
		Polar display of the relative co-ordinates on the status bar on/off.
		Display/entry of coordinates or dimensions in inches or millimeters.
		Change cursor display shape.
		Display general rats nest (incomplete connections between footprints).
		Display footprint rats nest dynamically as it is moved.
		Enable/Disable automatic deletion of a track when it is redrawn.
		Show filled areas in zones
		Do not show filled areas in zones
		Show only outlines of filled areas in zones
		Display of pads in outline mode on/off.
		Display of vias in outline mode on/off.
		Display of tracks in outline mode on/off.

	High contrast display mode on/off. In this mode the active layer is displayed normally, all the other layers are displayed in gray. Useful for working on multi-layer circuits.
	Hide/Show the Layers manager
	Access to microwaves tools. Under development

3.13 Pop-up windows and fast editing

A right-click of the mouse opens a pop-up window. Its contents depends on the element pointed at by the cursor. This gives immediate access to:

- Changing the display (centre display on cursor, zoom in or out or selecting the zoom).

- Setting the grid size.

- Additionally a right-click on an element enables editing of the most commonly modified element parameters.

The screenshots below show what the pop-up windows looks like.

3.14 Available modes

There are 3 modes when using pop-up menus. In the pop-up menus, these modes add or remove some specific commands.

and disabled	Normal mode
enabled	Footprint mode
enabled	Tracks mode

3.14.1 Normal mode

- Pop-up menu with no selection:

- Pop-up menu with track selected:

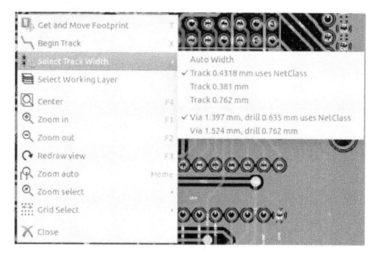

- Pop-up menu with footprint selected:

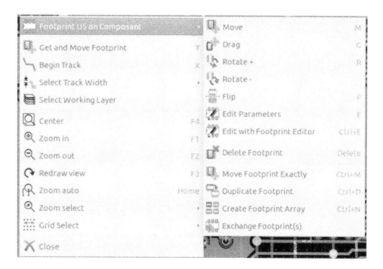

3.14.2 Footprint mode

Same cases in Footprint Mode (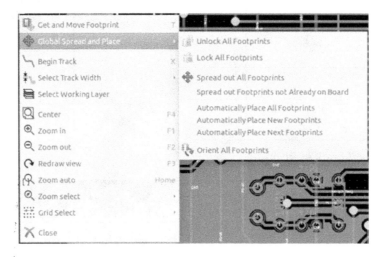 enabled)

- Pop-up menu with no selection:

- Pop-up menu with track selected:

- Pop-up menu with footprint selected:

3.14.3 Tracks mode

Same cases in Track Mode (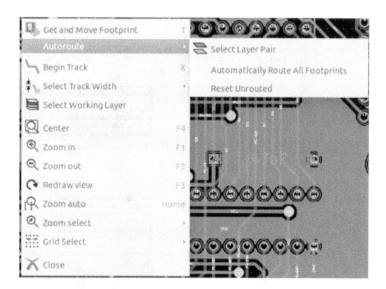 enabled)

- Pop-up menu with no selection:

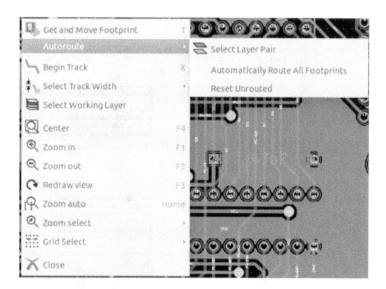

- Pop-up menu with track selected:

- Pop-up menu with footprint selected:

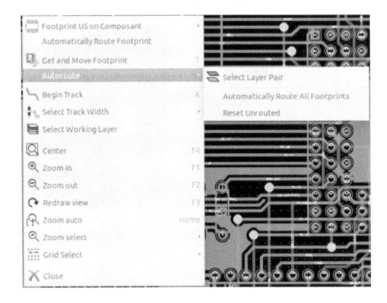

Chapter 4

Schematic Implementation

4.1 Linking a schematic to a printed circuit board

Generally speaking, a schematic sheet is linked to its printed circuit board by means of the netlist file, which is normally generated by the schematic editor used to make the schematic. Pcbnew accepts netlist files made with Eeschema or Orcad PCB 2. The netlist file, generated from the schematic is usually missing the footprints that correspond to the various components. Consequently an intermediate stage is necessary. During this intermediate process the association of components with footprints is performed. In KiCad, CvPcb is used to create this association and a file named *.cmp is produced. CvPcb also updates the netlist file using this information.

CvPcb can also output a "stuff file" *.stf which can be back annotated into the schematic file as the F2 field for each component, saving the task of re-assigning footprints in each schematic edit pass. In Eeschema copying a component will also copy the footprint assignment and set the reference designator as unassigned for later auto-incremental annotation.

Pcbnew reads the modified netlist file .net and, if it exists, the .cmp file. In the event of a footprint being changed directly in Pcbnew the .cmp file is automatically updated avoiding the requirement to run CvPcb again.

Refer to the figure of "Getting Started in KiCad" manual in the section *KiCad Workflow* that illustrates the work-flow of KiCad and how intermediate files are obtained and used by the different software tools that comprise KiCad.

4.2 Procedure for creating a printed circuit board

After having created your schematic in Eeschema:

- Generate the netlist using Eeschema.
- Assign each component in your netlist file to the corresponding land pattern (often called footprint) used on the printed circuit using Cvpcb.
- Launch Pcbnew and read the modified Netlist. This will also read the file with the footprint selections.

Pcbnew will then load automatically all the necessary footprints. Footprints can now be placed manually or automatically on the board and tracks can be routed.

4.3 Procedure for updating a printed circuit board

If the schematic is modified (after a printed circuit board has been generated), the following steps must be repeated:

- Generate a new netlist file using Eeschema.

- If the changes to the schematic involve new components, the corresponding footprints must be assigned using Cvpcb.

- Launch Pcbnew and re-read the modified netlist (this will also re-read the file with the footprint selections).

Pcbnew will then load automatically any new footprints, add the new connections and remove redundant connections. This process is called forward annotation and is a very common procedure when a PCB is made and updated.

4.4 Reading netlist file - loading footprints

4.4.1 Dialog box

Accessible from the icon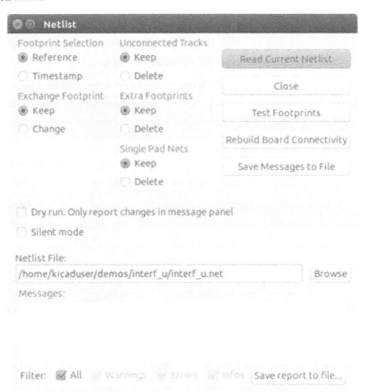

4.4.2 Available options

Footprint Selection	Components and corresponding footprints on board link: normal link is Reference (normal option Timestamp can be used after reannotation of schematic, if the previous annotation was destroyed (special option)
Exchange Footprint	If a footprint has changed in the netlist: keep old footprint or change to the new one.
Unconnected Tracks	Keep all existing tracks, or delete erroneous tracks
Extra Footprints	Remove footprints which are on board but not in the netlist. Footprint with attribute "Locked" will not be removed.
Single Pad Nets	Remove single pad nets.

4.4.3 Loading new footprints

With the GAL backend when new footprints are found in the netlist file, they will be loaded, spread out, and be ready for you to place as a group where you would like.

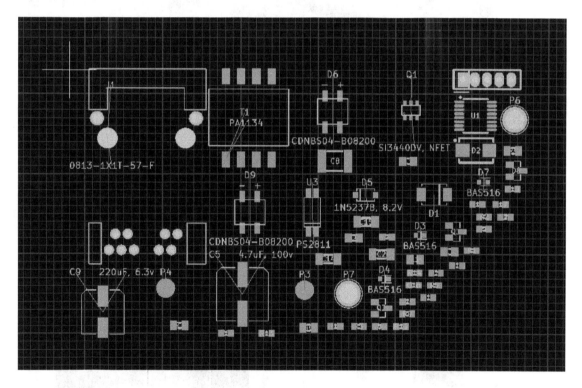

With the legacy backend when new footprints are found in the netlist file, they will be automatically loaded and placed at coordinate (0,0).

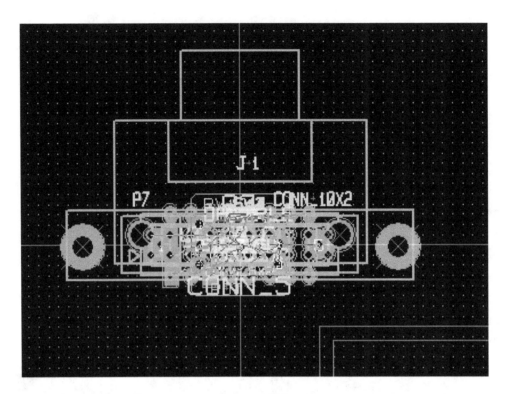

New footprints can be moved and arranged one by one. A better way is to automatically move (unstack) them:

Activate footprint mode ( )

Move the mouse cursor to a suitable (free of component) area, and click on the right button:

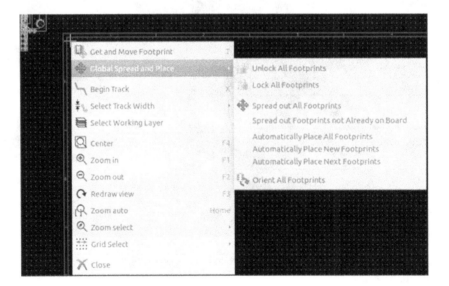

- Automatically Place New Footprints, if there is already a board with existing footprints.

- Automatically Place All Footprints, for the first time (when creating a board).

The following screenshot shows the results.

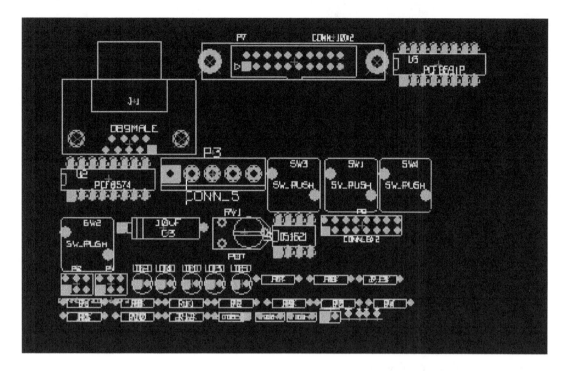

Chapter 5

Layers

5.1 Introduction

Pcbnew can work with 50 different layers:

- Between 1 and 32 copper layers for routing tracks.

- 14 fixed-purpose technical layers:

  - 12 paired layers (Front/Back): **Adhesive, Solder Paste, Silk Screen, Solder Mask, Courtyard, Fabrication**

  - 2 standalone layers: **Edge Cuts, Margin**

- 4 auxiliary layers that you can use any way you want: **Comments, E.C.O. 1, E.C.O. 2, Drawings**

5.2 Setting up layers

To open the **Layers Setup** from the menu bar, select **Design Rules** → **Layers Setup**.

The number of copper layers, their names, and their function are configured there. Unused technical layers can be disabled.

5.3 Layer Description

5.3.1 Copper Layers

Copper layers are the usual working layers used to place and re-arrange tracks. Layer numbers start from 0 (the first copper layer, on Front) and end at 31 (Back). Since components cannot be placed in **inner layers** (number 1 to 30), only layers number 0 and 31 are **component layer**.

The name of any copper layer is editable. Copper layers have a function attribute that is useful when using the external router *Freerouter*. Example of default layer names are **F.Cu** and **In0** for layer number 0.

5.3.2 Paired Technical Layers

12 technical layers come in pairs: one for the front, one for the back. You can recognize them with the "F." or "B." prefix in their names. The elements making up a footprint (pad, drawing, text) of one of these layers are automatically mirrored and moved to the complementary layer when the footprint is flipped.

The paired technical layers are:

Adhesive (F.Adhes and B.Adhes)
These are used in the application of adhesive to stick SMD components to the circuit board, generally before wave soldering.

Solder Paste (F.Paste and B.Paste)
Used to produce a mask to allow solder paste to be placed on the pads of surface mount components, generally before reflow soldering. Usually only surface mount pads occupy these layers.

Silk Screen (F.SilkS and B.SilkS)
They are the layers where the drawings of the components appear. That's where you draw things like component polarity, first pin indicator, reference for mounting, ⋯

Solder Mask (F.Mask and B.Mask)
These define the solder masks. All pads should appear on one of these layers (SMT) or both (for through hole) to prevent the varnish from covering the pads.

Courtyard (F.CrtYd and B.CrtYd)
Used to show how much space a component physically takes on the PCB.

Fabrication (F.Fab and B.Fab)
Footprint assembly (?).

5.3.3 Independant Technical Layers

Edge.Cuts
This layer is reserved for the drawing of circuit board outline. Any element (graphic, texts⋯) placed on this layer appears on all the other layers. Use this layer only to draw board outlines.

Margin
Board's edge setback outline (?).

5.3.4 Layers for general use

These layers are for any use. They can be used for text such as instructions for assembly or wiring, or construction drawings, to be used to create a file for assembly or machining. Their names are:

- Comments
- E.C.O. 1
- E.C.O. 2
- Drawings

5.4   Selection of the active layer

The selection of the active working layer can be done in several ways:

- Using the right toolbar (Layer manager).

- Using the upper toolbar.

- With the pop-up window (activated with the right mouse button).

- Using the + and - keys (works on copper layers only).

- By hot keys.

5.4.1   Selection using the layer manager

5.4.2 Selection using the upper toolbar

This directly selects the working layer.

Hot keys to select the working layer are displayed.

5.4.3 Selection using the pop-up window

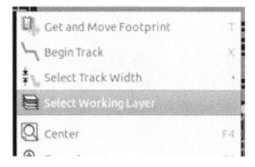

The Pop-up window opens a menu window which provides a choice for the working layer.

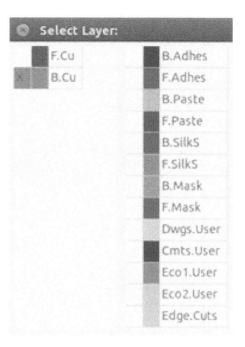

5.5   Selection of the Layers for Vias

If the **Add Tracks and Vias** icon is selected on the right hand toolbar, the Pop-Up window provides the option to change the layer pair used for vias:

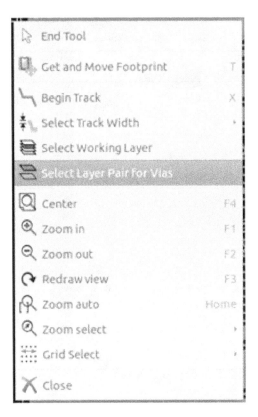

This selection opens a menu window which provides choice of the layers used for vias.

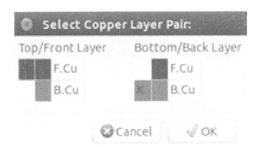

When a via is placed the working (active) layer is automatically switched to the alternate layer of the layer pair used for the vias.

One can also switch to another active layer by hot keys, and if a track is in progress, a via will be inserted.

5.6 Using the high-contrast mode

This mode is entered when the tool (in the left toolbar) is activated:

When using this mode, the active layer is displayed like in the normal mode, but all others layers are displayed in gray color.

There are two useful cases:

5.6.1   Copper layers in high-contrast mode

When a board uses more than four layers, this option allows the active copper layer to be seen more easily:

Normal mode (back side copper layer active):

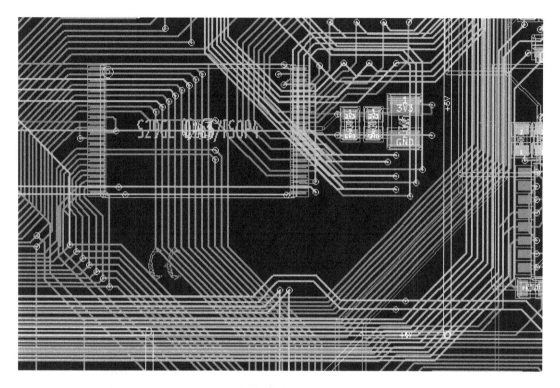

High-contrast mode (back side copper layer active):

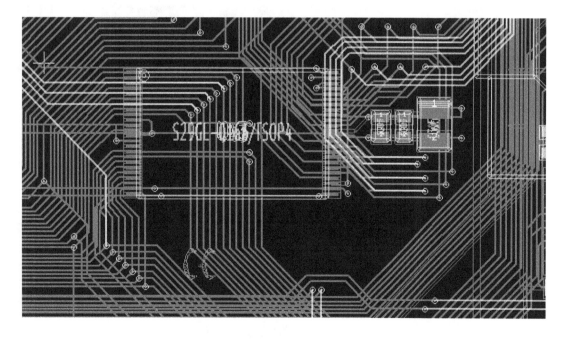

5.6.2 Technical layers

The other case is when it is necessary to examine solder paste layers and solder mask layers which are usually not displayed.

Masks on pads are displayed if this mode is active.

Normal mode (front side solder mask layer active):

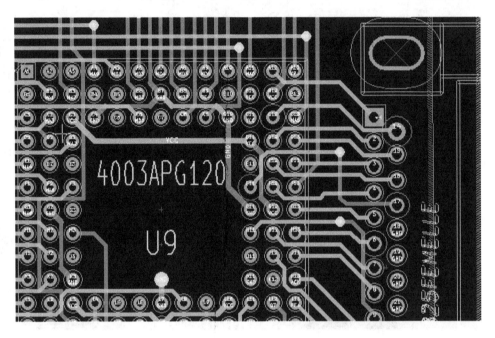

High-contrast mode (front side solder mask layer active):

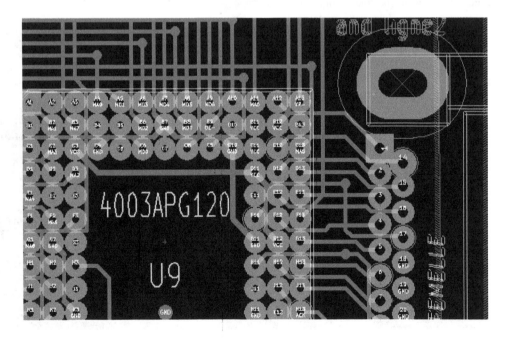

Chapter 6

Create and modify a board

6.1 Creating a board

6.1.1 Drawing the board outline

It is usually a good idea to define the outline of the board first. The outline is drawn as a sequence of line segments. Select *Edge.Cuts* as the active layer and use the *Add graphic line or polygon* tool to trace the edge, clicking at the position of each vertex and double-clicking to finish the outline. Boards usually have very precise dimensions, so it may be necessary to use the displayed cursor coordinates while tracing the outline. Remember that the relative coordinates can be zeroed at any time using the space bar, and that the display units can also be toggled using *Ctrl-U*. Relative coordinates enable very precise dimensions to be drawn. It is possible to draw a circular (or arc) outline:

1. Select the *Add graphic circle* or *Add graphic arc* tool

2. Click to fix the circle centre

3. Adjust the radius by moving the mouse

4. Finish by clicking again.

Note

The width of the outline can be adjusted in the Parameters menu (recommended width = 150 in 1/10 mils) or via the Options, but this will not be visible unless the graphics are displayed in other than outline mode.

The resulting outline might look something like this:

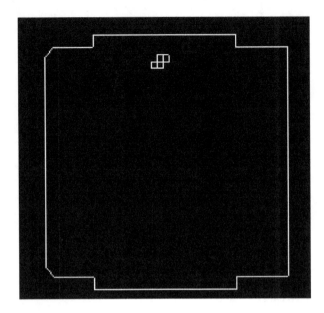

6.1.2 Using a DXF drawing for the board outline

As an alternative to drawing the board outline in Pcbnew directly, an outline can also be imported from a DXF drawing.

Using this feature allows for much more complex board shapes than is possible with the Pcbnew drawing capabilities.

For example a mechanical CAD package can be used to define a board shape that fits a particular enclosure.

6.1.2.1 Preparing the DXF drawing for import into KiCad

The **DXF** import capability in KiCad does not support DXF features like **POLYLINES** and **ELLIPSIS** and DXF files that use these features require a few conversion steps to prepare them for import.

A software package like LibreCAD can be used for this conversion.

As a first step, any **POLYLINES** need to be split (Exploded) into their original simpler shapes. In LibreCAD use the following steps:

1. Open a copy of the DXF file.

2. Select the board shape (selected shapes are shown with dashed lines).

3. In the **Modify** menu, select **Explode**.

4. Press ENTER.

As a next step, complex curves like **ELLIPSIS** need to be broken up in small line segments that *approximate* the required shape. This happens automatically when the DXF file is exported or saved in the older **DXF R12** file format (as the R12 format does not support complex curve shapes, CAD applications convert these shapes to line segments. Some CAD applications allow configuration of the number or the length of the line segments used). In LibreCAD the segment length it generally small enough for use in board shapes.

In LibreCAD, use the following steps to export to the **DXF R12** file format:

1. In the **File** menu, use **Save As···**

2. In the **Save Drawing As** dialog, there is a **Save as type:** selection near the bottom of the dialog. Select the option **Drawing Exchange DXF R12**.

3. Optionally enter a file name in the **File name:** field.

4. Click **Save**

Your DXF file is now ready for import into KiCad.

6.1.2.2 Importing the DXF file into KiCad

The following steps describe the import of the prepared DXF file as a board shape into KiCad. Note that the import bahaviour is slightly different depending on which *canvas* is used.

Using the "default" canvas mode:

1. In the **File** menu, select **Import** and then the **DXF File** option.

2. In the **Import DXF File** dialog use *Browse* to select the prepared DXF file to be imported.

3. In the *Place DXF origin (0,0) point:* option, select the placement of DXF origin relative to the board coordinates (the KiCad board has (0,0) in the top left corner). For the *User defined position* enter the coordinates in the *X Position* and *Y Position* fields.

4. In the *Layer* selection, select the board layer for the import. **Edge.Cuts** is needed for the board outline.

5. Click *OK*.

Using the "OpenGL" or "Cairo" canvas modes:

1. In the **File** menu, select **Import** and then the **DXF File** option.

2. In the **Import DXF File** dialog use *Browse* to select the prepared DXF file to be imported.

3. The *Place DXF origin (0,0) point:* option setting is ignored in this mode.

4. In the *Layer* selection, select the board layer for the import. **Edge.Cuts** is needed for the board outline.

5. Click *OK*.

6. The shape is now attached to your cursor and it can be moved around the board area.

7. Click to *drop* the shape on the board.

6.1.2.3 Example imported DXF shape

Here is an example of a DXF import with a board that had several elliptical segments approximated by a number of short line segments:

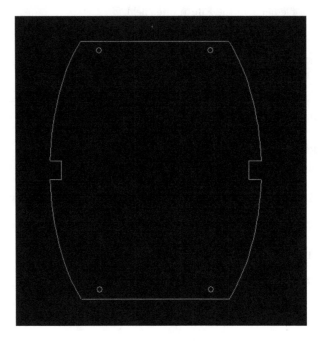

6.1.3 Reading the netlist generated from the schematic

Activate the icon to display the netlist dialog window:

If the name (path) of the netlist in the window title is incorrect, use the *Select* button to browse to the desired netlist. Then *Read* the netlist. Any footprints not already loaded will appear, superimposed one upon another (we shall see below how to move them automatically).

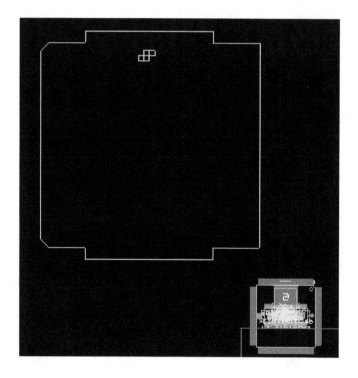

If none of the footprints have been placed, all of the footprints will appear on the board in the same place, making them difficult to recognize. It is possible to arrange them automatically (using the command *Global Spread and Place* accessed via the right mouse button). Here is the result of such automatic arrangement:

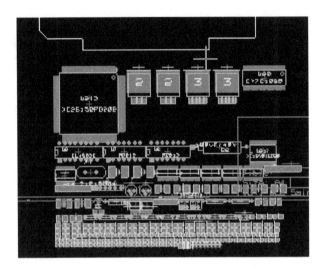

Note

If a board is modified by replacing an existing footprint with a new one (for example changing a 1/8W resistance to 1/2W) in CvPcb, it will be necessary to delete the existing component before Pcbnew will load the replacement footprint. However, if a footprint is to be replaced by an existing footprint, this is easier to do using the footprint dialog accessed by clicking the right mouse button over the footprint in question.

6.2 Correcting a board

It is very often necessary to correct a board following a corresponding change in the schematic.

6.2.1 Steps to follow

1. Create a new netlist from the modified schematic.

2. If new components have been added, link these to their corresponding footprint in CvPcb.

3. Read the new netlist in Pcbnew.

6.2.2 Deleting incorrect tracks

Pcbnew is able to automatically delete tracks that have become incorrect as a result of modifications. To do this, check the *Delete* option in the *Unconnected Tracks* box of the netlist dialog:

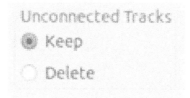

However, it is often quicker to modify such tracks by hand (the DRC function allows their identification).

6.2.3 Deleted components

Pcbnew can delete footprint corresponding to components that have been removed from the schematic. This is optional.

This is necessary because there are often footprints (holes for fixation screws, for instance) that are added to the PCB that never appear in the schematic.

If the "Extra Footprints" option is checked, a footprint corresponding to a component not found in the netlist will be deleted, unless they have the option "Locked" active. It is a good idea to activate this option for "mechanical" footprints:

6.2.4 Modified footprints

If a footprint is modified in the netlist (using CvPcb), but the footprint has already been placed, it will not be modified by Pcbnew, unless the corresponding option of the *Exchange Footprint* box of the netlist dialog is checked:

Changing a footprint (replacing a resistor with one of a different size, for instance) can be effected directly by editing the footprint.

6.2.5 Advanced options - selection using time stamps

Sometimes the notation of the schematic is changed, without any material changes in the circuit (this would concern the references - like R5, U4···).The PCB is therefore unchanged (except possibly for the silkscreen markings). Nevertheless, internally, components and footprints are represented by their reference. In this situation, the *Timestamp* option of the netlist dialog may be selected before re-reading the netlist:

With this option, Pcbnew no longer identifies footprints by their reference, but by their time stamp instead. The time stamp is automatically generated by Eeschema (it is the time and date when the component was placed in the schematic).

 Warning

Great care should be exercised when using this option (save the file first!). This is because the technique is complicated in the case of components containing multiple parts (e.g. a 7400 has 4 parts and one case). In this situation, the time stamp is not uniquely defined (for the 7400 there would be up to four - one for each part). Nevertheless, the time stamp option usually resolves re-annotation problems.

6.3 Direct exchange for footprints already placed on board

Changing a footprint (or some identical footprints) to another footprint is very useful, and is very easy:

1. Click on a footprint to open the Edit dialog box.

2. Activate Change Footprints.

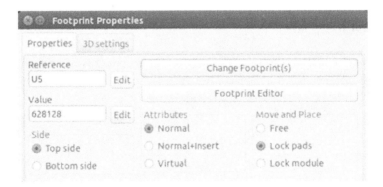

Options for Change Footprint(s):

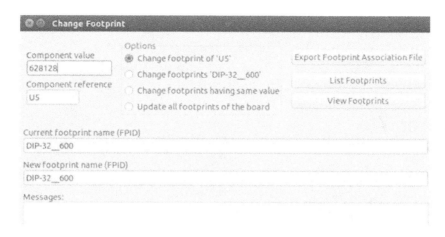

One must choose a new footprint name and use:

- **Change footprint of** *xx* for the current footprint

- **Change footprints** *yy* for all footprints like the current footprint.

- **Change footprints having same value** for all footprints like the current footprint, restricted to components which have the same value.

- **Update all footprints of the board** for reloading of all footprints on board.

Chapter 7

Footprint placement

7.1 Assisted placement

Whilst moving footprints the footprint ratsnest (the net connections) can be displayed to assist the placement. To

enable this the icon ![icon] of the left toolbar must be activated.

7.2 Manual placement

Select the footprint with the right mouse button then choose the Move command from the menu. Move the footprint to the required position and place it with the left mouse button. If required the selected footprint can also be rotated, inverted or edited. Select Cancel from the menu (or press the Esc key) to abort.

Here you can see the display of the footprint ratsnest during a move:

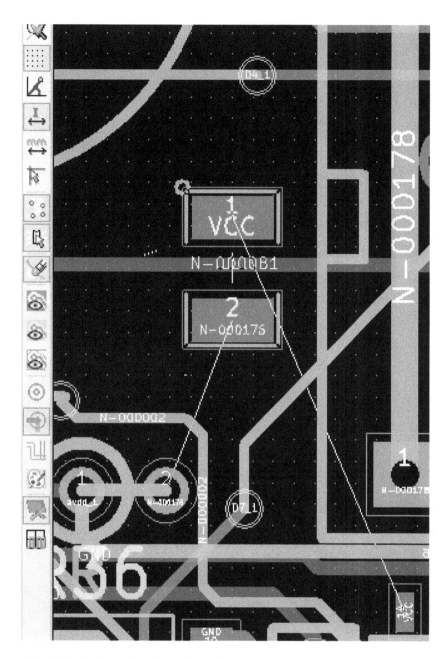

The circuit once all the footprints are placed may be as shown:

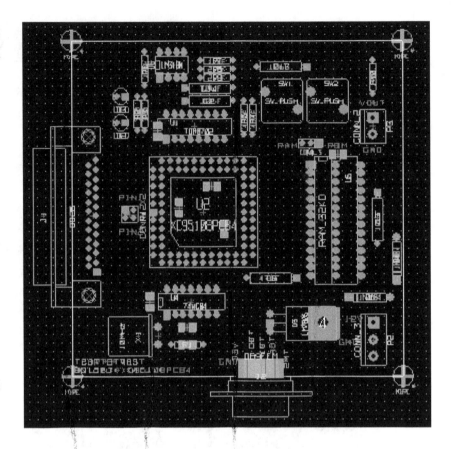

7.3 Automatic Footprint Distribution

Generally speaking, footprints can only be moved if they have not been "Fixed". This attribute can be turned on and off from the pop-up window (click right mouse button over footprint) whilst in Footprint Mode, or through the Edit Footprint Menu.

As stated in the last chapter, new footprints loaded during the reading of the netlist appear piled up at a single location on the board. Pcbnew allows an automatic distribution of the footprints to make manual selection and placement easier.

- Select the option "Footprint Mode" (Icon ![icon] on the upper toolbar).

- The pop-up window activated by the right mouse button becomes:

If there is a footprint under the cursor:

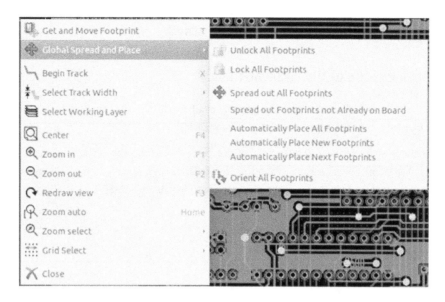

If there is nothing under the cursor:

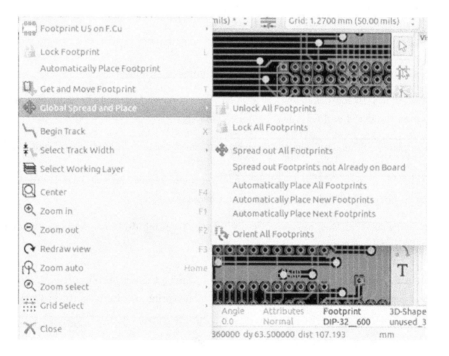

In both cases the following commands are available:

- **Spread out All Footprints** allows the automatic distribution of all the footprints not Fixed. This is generally used after the first reading of a netlist.

- **Spread out Footprints not Already on Board** allows the automatic distribution of the footprints which have not been placed already within the PCB outline. This command requires that an outline of the board has been drawn to determine which footprints can be automatically distributed.

7.4 Automatic placement of footprints

7.4.1 Characteristics of the automatic placer

The automatic placement feature allows the placement of footprints onto the 2 faces of the circuit board (however switching a footprint onto the copper layer is not automatic).

It also seeks the best orientation (0, 90, -90, 180 degrees) of the footprint. The placement is made according to an optimization algorithm, which seeks to minimize the length of the ratsnest, and which seeks to create space between the larger footprints with many pads. The order of placement is optimized to initially place these larger footprints with many pads.

7.4.2 Preparation

Pcbnew can thus place the footprints automatically, however it is necessary to guide this placement, because no software can guess what the user wants to achieve.

Before an automatic placement is carried out one must:

- Create the outline of the board (It can be complex, but it must be closed if the form is not rectangular).

- Manually place the components whose positions are imposed (Connectors, clamp holes, etc).

- Similarly, certain SMD footprints and critical components (large footprints for example) must be on a specific side or position on the board and this must be done manually.

- Having completed any manual placement these footprints must be "Fixed" to prevent them being moved. With the Footprint Mode icon selected right click on the footprint and pick "Fix Footprint" on the Pop-up menu. This can also be done through the Edit/Footprint Pop-up menu.

- Automatic placement can then be carried out. With the Footprint Mode icon selected, right click and select Glob(al) Move and Place - then Autoplace All Footprints.

During automatic placement, if required, Pcbnew can optimize the orientation of the footprints. However rotation will only be attempted if this has been authorized for the footprint (see Edit Footprint Options).

Usually resistors and non-polarized capacitors are authorized for 180 degrees rotation. Some footprints (small transistors for example) can be authorized for +/- 90 and 180 degrees rotation.

For each footprint one slider authorizes 90 degree Rot(ation) and a second slider authorizes 180 degree Rot(ation). A setting of 0 prevents rotation, a setting of 10 authorizes it, and an intermediate value indicates a preference for/ against rotation.

The rotation authorization can be done by editing the footprint once it is placed on the board. However it is preferable to set the required options to the footprint in the library as these settings will then be inherited each time the footprint is used.

7.4.3 Interactive auto-placement

It may be necessary during automatic placement to stop (press Esc key) and manually re-position a footprint. Using the command Autoplace Next Footprint will restart the autoplacement from the point at which it was stopped.

The command Autoplace new footprints allows the automatic placement of the footprints which have not been placed already within the PCB outline. It will not move those within the PCB outline even if they are not "fixed".

The command Autoplace Footprint makes it possible to execute an autoplacement on the footprint pointed to by the mouse, even if its *fixed* attribute is active.

7.4.4 Additional note

Pcbnew automatically determines the possible zone of placement of the footprints by respecting the shape of the board outline, which is not necessarily rectangular (It can be round, or have cutouts, etc).

If the board is not rectangular, the outline must be closed, so that Pcbnew can determine what is inside and what is outside the outline. In the same way, if there are internal cutouts, their outline will have to be closed.

Pcbnew calculates the possible zone of placement of the footprints using the outline of the board, then passes each footprint in turn over this area in order to determine the optimum position at which to place it.

Chapter 8

Setting routing parameters

8.1 Current settings

8.1.1 Accessing the main dialog

The most important parameters are accessed from the following drop-down menu:

and are set in the Design Rules dialog.

8.1.2 Current settings

Current settings are displayed in the top toolbar.

8.2 General options

The General options menu is available via the top toolbar link Preferences → General dialog.

The dialog looks like the following:

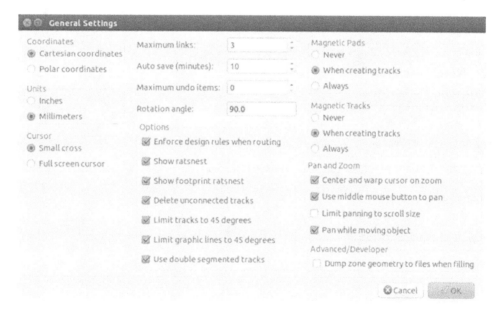

For the creation of tracks the necessary parameters are:

- **Tracks 45 Only**: Directions allowed for track segments are 0, 45 or 90 degrees.

- **Double Segm Track**: When creating tracks, 2 segments will be displayed.

- **Tracks Auto Del**: When recreating tracks, the old one will be automatically deleted if considered redundant.

- **Magnetic Pads**: The graphic cursor becomes a pad, centered in the pad area.

- **Magnetic Tracks**: The graphic cursor becomes the track axis.

8.3 Netclasses

Pcbnew allows you to define different routing parameters for each net. Parameters are defined by a group of nets.

- A group of nets is called a Netclass.
- There is always a netclass called "default".
- Users can add other Netclasses.

A netclass specifies:

- The width of tracks, via diameters and drills.
- The clearance between pads and tracks (or vias).
- When routing, Pcbnew automatically selects the netclass corresponding to the net of the track to create or edit, and therefore the routing parameters.

8.3.1 Setting routing parameters

The choice is made in the menu: Design Rules → Design Rules.

8.3.2 Netclass editor

The Netclass editor allows you to:

- Add or delete Netclasses.
- Set routing parameters values: clearance, track width, via sizes.
- Group nets in netclasses.

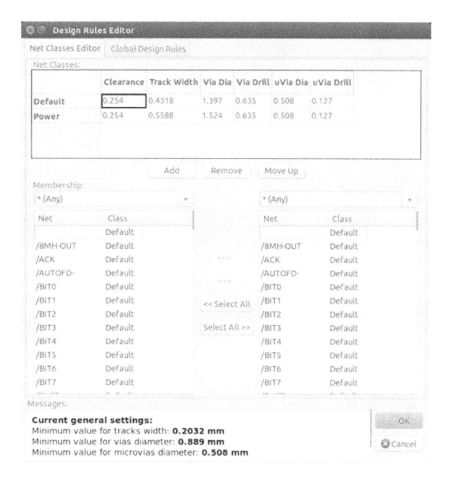

8.3.3 Global Design Rules

The global design rules are:

- Enabling/disabling Blind/buried Vias use.

- Enabling/disabling Micro Vias use.

- Minimum Allowed Values for tracks and vias.

A DRC error is raised when a value smaller than the minimum value specified is encountered. The second dialog panel is:

This dialog also allows to enter a "stock" of tracks and via sizes.

When routing, one can select one of these values to create a track or via, instead of using the netclass's default value.

Useful in critical cases when a small track segment must have a specific size.

8.3.4 Via parameters

Pcbnew handles 3 types of vias:

- Through vias (usual vias).

- Blind or buried vias.

- Micro Vias, like buried vias but restricted to an external layer to its nearest neighbor. They are intended to connect BGA pins to the nearest inner layer. Their diameter is usually very small and they are drilled by laser.

By default, all vias have the same drill value.

This dialog specifies the smallest acceptable values for via parameters. On a board, a via smaller than specified here generates a DRC error.

8.3.5 Track parameters

Specify the minimum acceptable track width. On a board, a track width smaller than specified here generates a DRC error.

8.3.6 Specific sizes

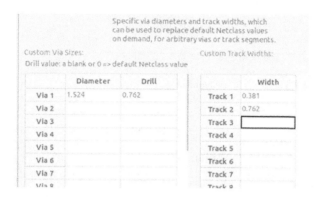

One can enter a set of extra tracks and/or via sizes. While routing a track, these values can be used on demand instead of the values from the current netclass values.

8.4 Examples and typical dimensions

8.4.1 Track width

Use the largest possible value and conform to the minimum sizes given here.

Units	CLASS 1	CLASS 2	CLASS 3	CLASS 4	CLASS 5
mm	0.8	0.5	0.4	0.25	0.15
mils	31	20	16	10	6

8.4.2 Insulation (clearance)

Units	CLASS 1	CLASS 2	CLASS 3	CLASS 4	CLASS 5
mm	0.7	0.5	0.35	0.23	0.15
mils	27	20	14	9	6

Usually, the minimum clearance is very similar to the minimum track width.

8.5 Examples

8.5.1 Rustic

- Clearance: 0.35 mm (0.0138 inches).

- Track width: 0.8 mm (0.0315 inches).

- Pad diameter for ICs and vias: 1.91 mm (0.0750 inches).

- Pad diameter for discrete components: 2.54 mm (0.1 inches).

- Ground track width: 2.54 mm (0.1 inches).

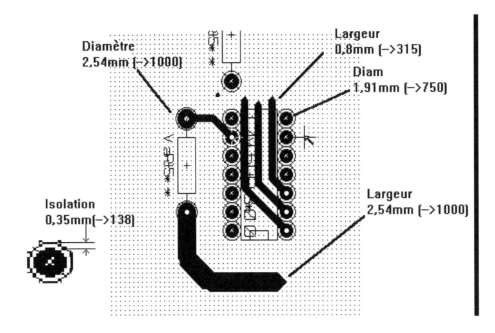

8.5.2 Standard

- Clearance: 0.35mm (0.0138 inches).

- Track width: 0.5mm (0.0127 inches).

- Pad diameter for ICs: make them elongated in order to allow tracks to pass between IC pads and yet have the pads offer a sufficient adhesive surface (1.27 x 2.54 mm -→ 0.05 x 0.1 inches).

- Vias: 1.27 mm (0.0500 inches).

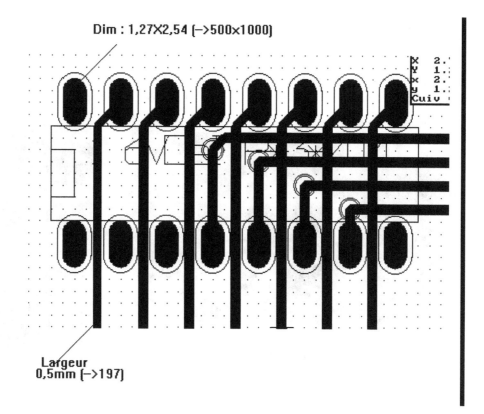

8.6   Manual routing

Manual routing is often recommended, because it is the only method offering control over routing priorities. For example, it is preferable to start by routing power tracks, making them wide and short and keeping analog and digital supplies well separated. Later, sensitive signal tracks should be routed. Amongst other problems, automatic routing often requires many vias. However, automatic routing can offer a useful insight into the positioning of footprints. With experience, you will probably find that the automatic router is useful for quickly routing the *obvious* tracks, but the remaining tracks will best be routed by hand.

8.7   Help when creating tracks

Pcbnew can display the full ratsnest, if the button is activated.

The button allows one to highlight a net (click to a pad or an existing track to highlight the corresponding net).

The DRC checks tracks in real time while creating them. One cannot create a track which does not match the DRC rules. It is possible to disable the DRC by clicking on the button. This is, however, not recommended, use it only in specific cases.

8.7.1 Creating tracks

A track can be created by clicking on the button 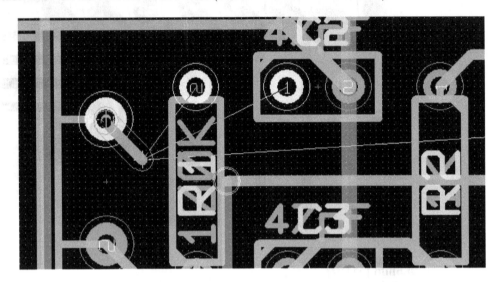. A new track must start on a pad or on another track, because Pcbnew must know the net used for the new track (in order to match the DRC rules).

When creating a new track, Pcbnew shows links to nearest unconnected pads, link number set in option "Max. Links" in General Options.

End the track by double-clicking, by the pop-up menu or by its hot key.

8.7.2 Moving and dragging tracks

When the button 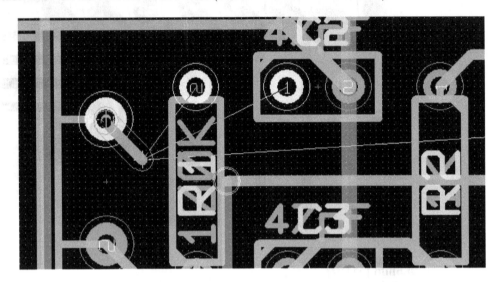 is active, the track where the cursor is positioned can be moved with the hotkey M. If you want to drag the track you can use the hotkey G.

8.7.3 Via Insertion

A via can be inserted only when a track is in progress:

- By the pop-up menu.

- By the hotkey *V*.

- By switching to a new copper layer using the appropriate hotkey.

8.8 Select/edit the track width and via size

When clicking on a track or a pad, Pcbnew automatically selects the corresponding Netclass, and the track size and via dimensions are derived from this netclass.

As previously seen, the Global Design Rules editor has a tool to insert extra tracks and via sizes.

- The horizontal toolbar can be used to select a size.

- When the button   is active, the current track width can be selected from the pop-up menu (accessible as well when creating a track).

- The user can utilize the default Netclasses values or a specified value.

8.8.1 Using the horizontal toolbar

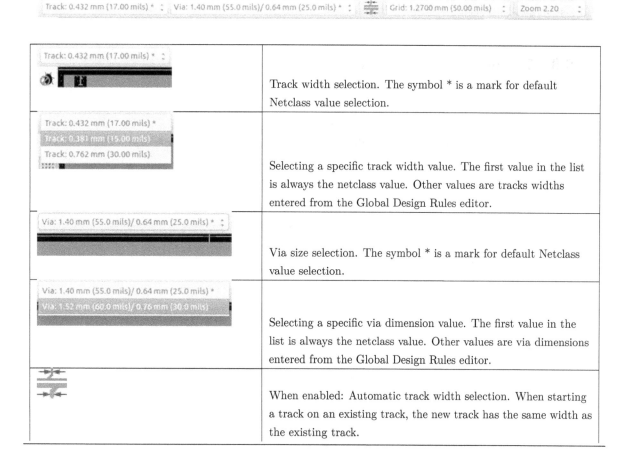

Track: 0.432 mm (17.00 mils) *	Track width selection. The symbol * is a mark for default Netclass value selection.
Track: 0.432 mm (17.00 mils) * Track: 0.381 mm (15.00 mils) Track: 0.762 mm (30.00 mils)	Selecting a specific track width value. The first value in the list is always the netclass value. Other values are tracks widths entered from the Global Design Rules editor.
Via: 1.40 mm (55.0 mils)/ 0.64 mm (25.0 mils) *	Via size selection. The symbol * is a mark for default Netclass value selection.
Via: 1.40 mm (55.0 mils)/ 0.64 mm (25.0 mils) * Via: 1.52 mm (60.0 mils)/ 0.76 mm (30.0 mils)	Selecting a specific via dimension value. The first value in the list is always the netclass value. Other values are via dimensions entered from the Global Design Rules editor.
	When enabled: Automatic track width selection. When starting a track on an existing track, the new track has the same width as the existing track.

| 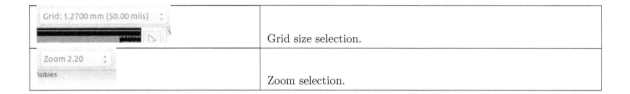 | Grid size selection. |
| | Zoom selection. |

8.8.2 Using the pop-up menu

One can select a new size for routing, or change to a previously created via or track segment:

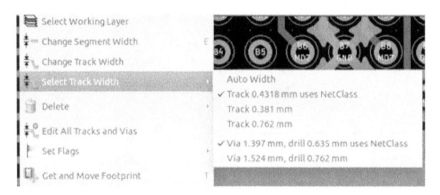

If you want to change many via (or track) sizes, the best way is to use a specific Netclass for the net(s) that must be edited (see global changes).

8.9 Editing and changing tracks

8.9.1 Change a track

In many cases redrawing a track is required.

New track (in progress):

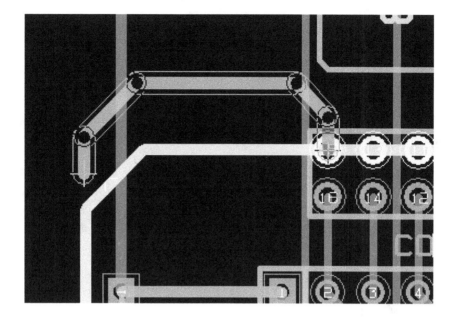

When finished:

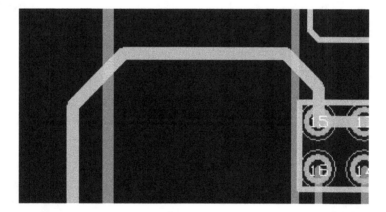

Pcbnew will automatically remove the old track if it is redundant.

8.9.2 Global changes

Global tracks and via sizes dialog editor is accessible via the pop-up window by right clicking on a track:

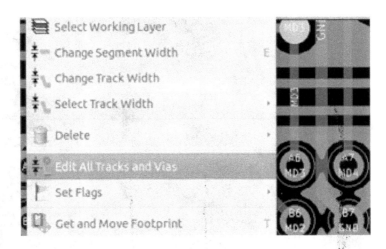

The dialog editor allows global changes of tracks and/or vias for:

- The current net.

- The whole board.

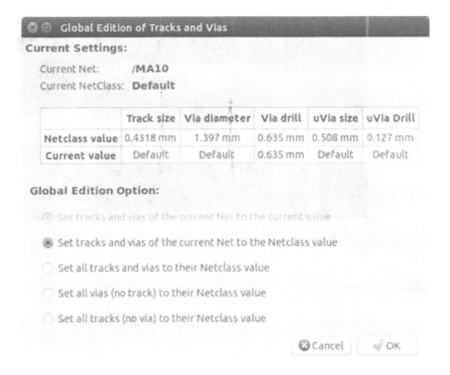

Chapter 9

Interactive Router

The Interactive Router lets you quickly and efficiently route your PCBs by shoving off or walking around items on the PCB that collide with the trace you are currently drawing.

Following modes are supported:

- **Highlight collisions**, which highlights all violating objects with a nice, shiny green color and shows violating clearance regions.

- **Shove**, attempting to push and shove all items colliding with the currently routed track.

- **Walk around**, trying to avoid obstacles by hugging/walking around them.

9.1 Setting up

Before using the Interactive Router, please set up these two things:

- **Clearance settings** To set the clearances, open the *Design Rules* dialog and make sure at least the default clearance value looks sensible.

- **Enable OpenGL mode** By selecting *View→Switch canvas to OpenGL* menu option or pressing **F11**.

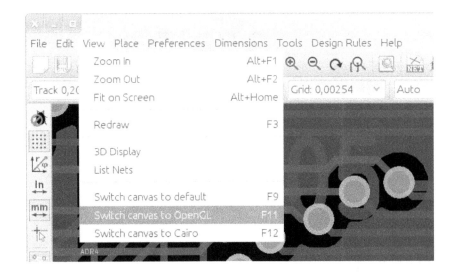

9.2 Laying out tracks

To activate the router tool press the *Interactive Router* button ⌐ or the **X** key. The cursor will turn into a cross and the tool name, will appear in the status bar.

To start a track, click on any item (a pad, track or a via) or press the **X** key again hovering the mouse over that item. The new track will use the net of the starting item. Clicking or pressing **X** on empty PCB space starts a track with no net assigned.

Move the mouse to define shape of the track. The router will try to follow the mouse trail, hugging unmovable obstacles (such as pads) and shoving colliding traces/vias, depending on the mode. Retreating the mouse cursor will cause the shoved items to spring back to their former locations.

Clicking on a pad/track/via in the same net finishes routing. Clicking in empty space fixes the segments routed so far and continues routing the trace.

In order to stop routing and undo all changes (shoved items, etc.), simply press **Esc**.

Pressing **V** or selecting *Place Through Via* from the context menu while routing a track attaches a via at the end of the trace being routed. Pressing **V** again disables via placement. Clicking in any spot establishes the via and continues routing.

Pressing / or selecting *Switch Track Posture* from the context menu toggles the direction of the initial track segment between straight or diagonal.

Note

By default, the router snaps to centers/axes of the items. Snapping can be disabled by holding **Shift** while routing or selecting items.

9.3 Setting track widths and via sizes

There are several ways to pre-select a track width/via size or to change it during routing:

- Use standard KiCad shortcuts.

- Press **W** or select *Custom Track Width* from the context menu to type in a custom track width/via size.

- Pick a predefined width from the *Select Track Width* sub-menu of the context menu.

- Select *Use the starting track width* in the *Select Track Width* menu to pick the width from the start item (or the traces already connected to it).

9.4 Dragging

The router can drag track segments, corners and vias. To drag an item, click on it with **Ctrl** key pressed, hover the mouse and press **G** or select *Drag Track/Via* from the context menu. Finish dragging by clicking again or abort by pressing *Esc*.

9.5   Options

The router behavior can be configured by pressing *E* or selecting *Routing Options* from the context menu while in the Track mode. It opens a window like the one below:

The options are:

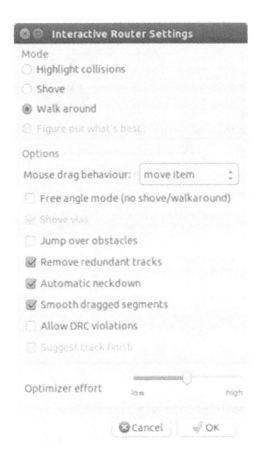

- **Mode** - select how the router handles DRC violation (shoving, walking around, etc.)

- **Shove vias** - when disabled, vias are treated as un-movable objects and hugged instead of shoved.

- **Jump over obstacles** - when enabled, the router tries to move colliding traces behind solid obstacles (e.g. pads) instead of "reflecting" back the collision

- **Remove redundant tracks** - removes loops while routing (e.g. if the new track ensures same connectivity as an already existing one, the old track is removed). Loop removal works locally (only between the start and end of the currently routed trace).

- **Automatic neckdown** - when enabled, the router tries to break out pads/vias in a clean way, avoiding acute angles and jagged breakout traces.

- **Smooth dragged segments** - when enabled, the router attempts to merge several jagged segments into a single straight one (dragging mode).

- **Allow DRC violations** (*Highlight collisions* mode only) - allows to establish a track even if is violating the DRC rules.

- **Optimizer effort** - defines how much time the router shall spend optimizing the routed/shoved traces. More effort means cleaner routing (but slower), less effort means faster routing but somewhat jagged traces.

Chapter 10

Creating copper zones

Copper zones are defined by an outline (closed polygon), and can include holes (closed polygons inside the outline). A zone can be drawn on a copper layer or alternatively on a technical layer.

10.1 Creating zones on copper layers

Pad (and track) connections to filled copper areas are checked by the DRC engine. A zone must be filled (not just created) to connect pads. Pcbnew currently uses track segments or polygons to fill copper areas.

Each option has its advantages and its disadvantages, the main disadvantage being increased screen redraw time on slower machines. The final result is however the same.

For calculation time reasons, the zone filling is not recreated after each change, but only:

- If a filling zone command is executed.

- When a DRC test is performed.

Copper zones must be filled or refilled after changes in tracks or pads are made. Copper zones (usually ground and power planes) are usually attached to a net.

In order to create a copper zone you should:

- Select parameters (net name, layer···). Turning on the layer and highlighting this net is not mandatory but it is good practice.

- Create the zone limit (If not, the entire board will be filled.).

- Fill the zone.

Pcbnew tries to fill all zones in one piece, and usually, there will be no unconnected copper blocks. It can happen that some areas remain unfilled. Zones having no net are not cleaned and can have insulated areas.

10.2   Creating a zone

10.2.1   Creating the limits of a zone

Use the tool 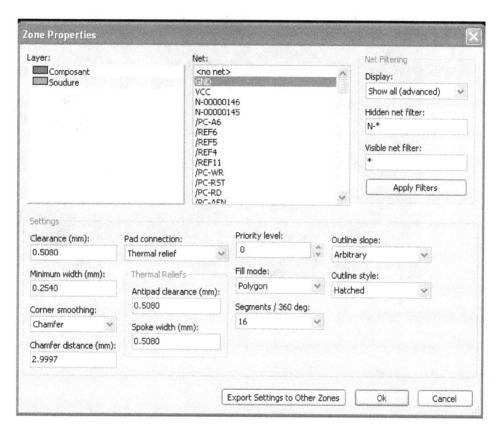. The active layer must be a copper layer. When clicking to start the zone outline, the following dialog box will be opened.

You can specify all parameters for this zone:

- Net

- Layer

- Filling options

- Pad options

- Priority level

Draw the zone limit on this layer. This zone limit is a polygon, created by left-clicking at each corner. A double-click will end and close the polygon. If the starting point and ending point are not at the same coordinate, Pcbnew will add a segment from the end point to the start point.

Note

- The DRC control is active when creating zone outlines.

- A corner which creates a DRC error will not be accepted by Pcbnew.

In the following image you can see an example of a zone limit (polygon in thin hatched line):

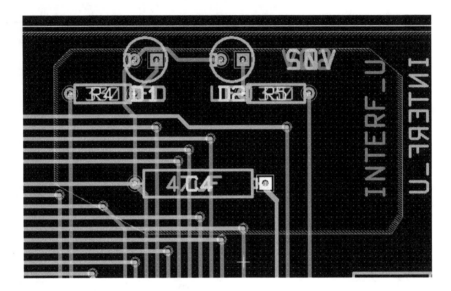

10.2.2 Priority level

Sometimes a small zone must be created inside a large zone.

This is possible if the small zone has a higher priority level than the large zone.

Level setting:

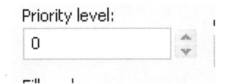

Here is an example:

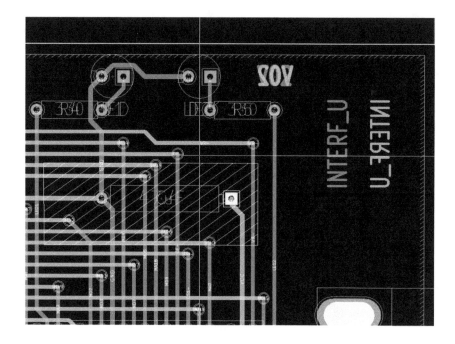

After filling:

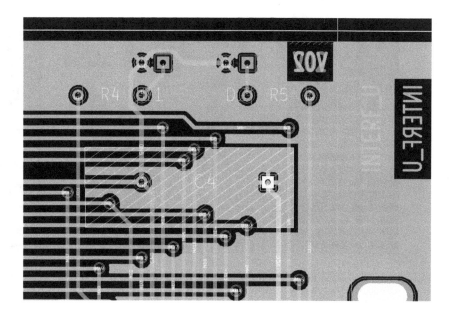

10.2.3 Filling the zone

When filling a zone, Pcbnew removes all unconnected copper islands. To access the zone filling command, right-click on the edge zone.

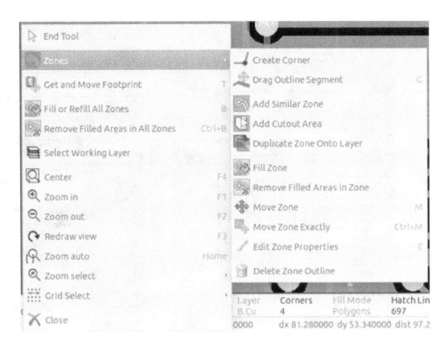

Activate the "Fill Zone" command. Below is the filling result for a starting point inside the polygon:

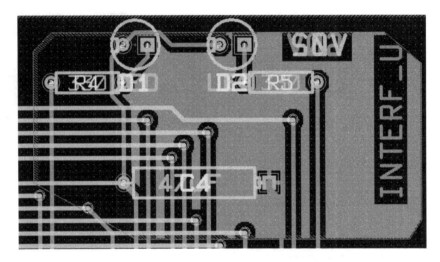

The polygon is the border of the filling area. You can see a non-filled area inside the zone, because this area is not accessible:

- A track creates a border, and

- There is no starting point for filling in this area.

Note

You can use many polygons to create cutout areas. Here you can see an example:

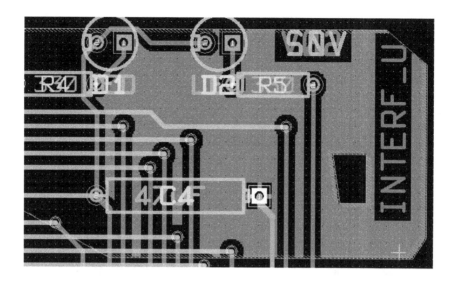

10.3   Filling options

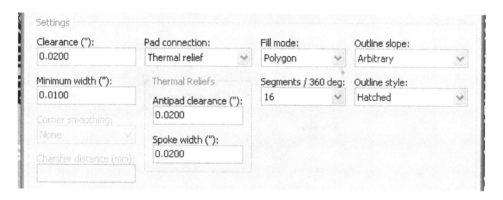

When you fill an area, you must choose:

- The mode for filling.

- The clearance and minimum copper thickness.

- How pads are drawn inside the zone (or connected to this zone).

- Thermal relief parameters.

10.3.1   Filling mode

Zones can be filled using polygons or segments. The result is the same. If you have problems with polygon mode (slow screen refresh) you should use segments.

10.3.2 Clearance and minimum copper thickness

A good choice for clearance is a grid that is a bit bigger than the routing grid. Minimum copper thickness value ensures that there are no too small copper ares.

 Warning

if this value is too large, small shapes like thermal stubs in thermal reliefs cannot be drawn.

10.3.3 Pad options

Pads of the net can either be included or excluded from the zone, or connected by thermal reliefs.

- If included, soldering and un-soldering can be very difficult due to the high thermal mass of the large copper area.

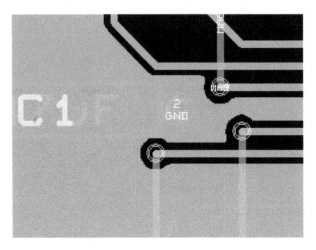

- If excluded, the connection to the zone will not be very good.

    - The zone can be filled only if tracks exists to connect zone areas.
    - Pads must be connected by tracks.

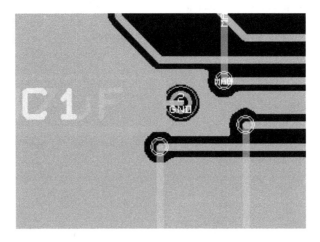

- A thermal relief is a good compromise.

  - Pad is connected by 4 track segments.
  - The segment width is the current value used for the track width.

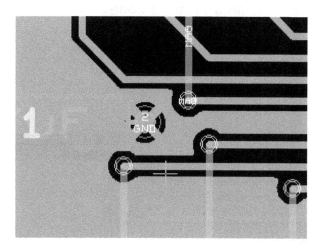

10.3.4 Thermal relief parameters

You can set two parameters for thermal reliefs:

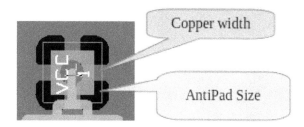

10.3.5 Choice of parameters

The copper width value for thermal reliefs must be bigger than the minimum thickness value for the copper zone. If not, they cannot be drawn.

Additionally, a too large value for this parameter or for antipad size does not allow one to create a thermal relief for small pads (like pad sizes used for SMD components).

10.4 Adding a cutout area inside a zone

A zone must already exist. To add a cutout area (a non-filled area inside the zone):

- Right-click on an existing edge outline.
- Select Add Cutout Area.

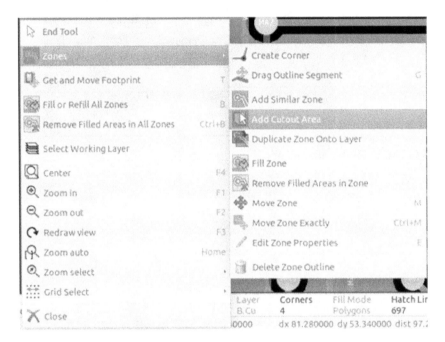

- Create the new outline.

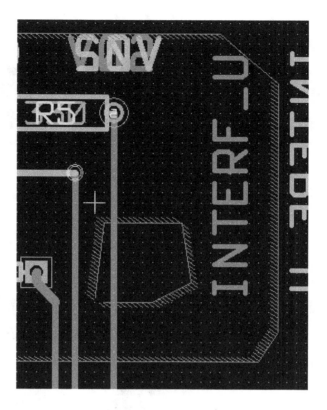

10.5 Outlines editing

An outline can be modified by:

- Moving a corner or an edge.

- Deleting or adding a corner.

- Adding a similar zone, or a cutout area.

If polygons are overlapping they will be combined.

To do that, right-click on a corner or on an edge, then select the proper command.

Here is a corner (from a cutout) that has been moved:

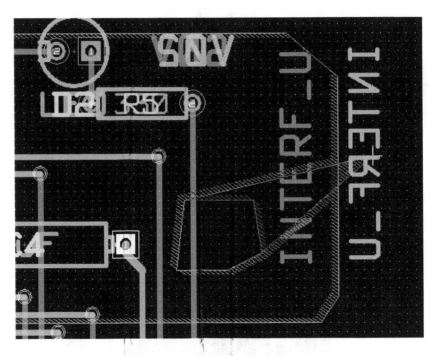

Here is the final result:

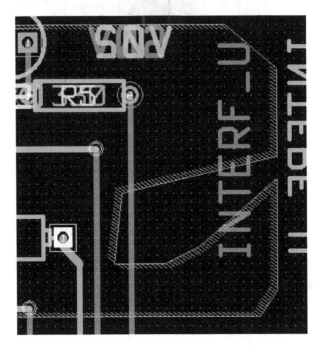

Polygons are combined.

10.5.1 Adding a similar zone

Adding the similar zone:

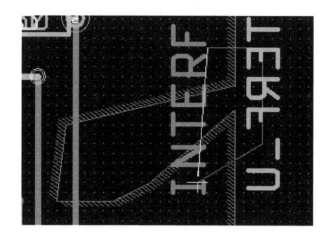

Final result:

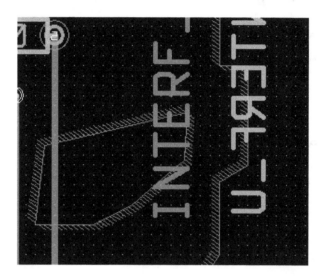

10.6   Editing zone parameters

When right-clicking on an outline, and using *Edit Zone Params* the Zone params Dialog box will open. Initial parameters can be inputted . If the zone is already filled, refilling it will be necessary.

10.7   Final zone filling

When the board is finished, one must fill or refill all zones. To do this:

- Activate the tool zones via the button .

- Right-click to display the pop-up menu.

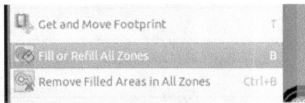

- Use Fill or Refill All Zones:

 Warning

Calculation can take some time if the filling grid is small.

10.8 Change zones net names

After editing a schematic, you can change the name of any net. For instance VCC can be changed to +5V.

When a global DRC control is made Pcbnew checks if the zone net name exists, and displays an error if not.

Manually editing the zone parameters will be necessary to change the old name to the new one.

10.9 Creating zones on technical layers

10.9.1 Creating zone limits

This is done using the button [image]. The active layer must be a technical layer.

When clicking to start the zone outline, this dialog box is opened:

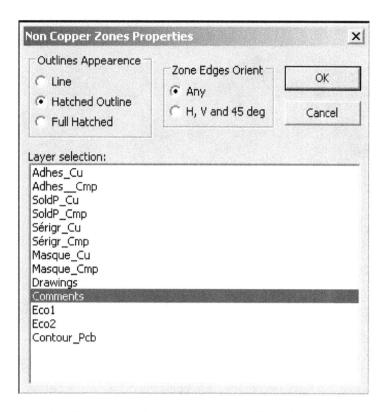

Select the technical layer to place the zone and draw the zone outline like explained previously for copper layers.

Note

- For editing outlines use the same method as for copper zones.

- If necessary, cutout areas can be added.

10.10 Creating a Keepout area

Select the tool

The active layer should be a copper layer.

After clicking on the starting point of a new keepout area, the dialog box is opened:

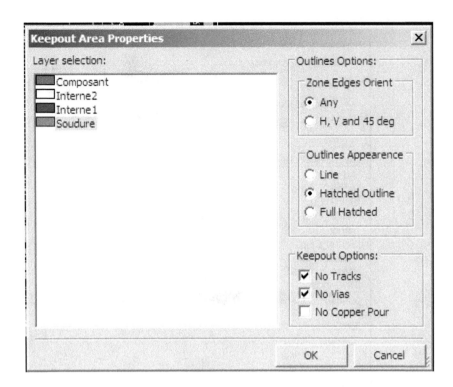

One can select disallowed items:

- Tracks.

- Vias.

- Copper pours.

When a track or a via is inside a keepout which does not allow it, a DRC error will be raised.

For copper zones, the area inside a keepout with no copper pour will be not filled. A keep-out area is a like a zone, so editing its outline is analogous to copper zone editing.

Chapter 11

Files for circuit fabrication

Let us see now what the steps are for the creation of the necessary files for the production of your printed circuit board.

All files generated by KiCad are placed in the working directory which is the same directory that contains the xxxx.brd file for the printed circuit board.

11.1 Final preparations

The generation of the necessary files for the production of your printed circuit board includes the following preparatory steps.

- Mark any layer (e.g., *top or front* and *bottom or back*) with the project name by placing appropriate text upon each of the layers.

- All text on copper layers (sometimes called *solder* or *bottom*) must be mirrored.

- Create any ground planes, modifying traces as required to ensure they are contiguous.

- Place alignment crosshairs and possibly the dimensions of the board outline (these are usually placed on one of the general purpose layers).

Here is an example showing all of these elements, except ground planes, which have been omitted for better visibility:

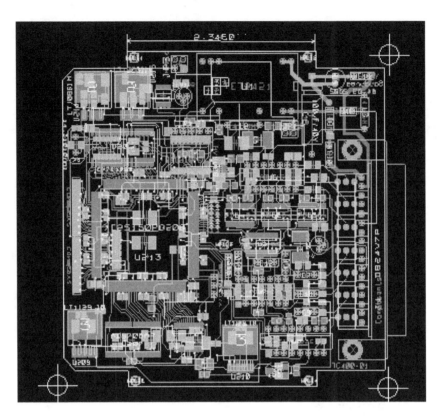

A color key for the 4 copper layers has also been included:

11.2   Final DRC test

Before generating the output files, a global DRC test is very strongly recommended.

Zones are filled or refilled when starting a DRC. Press the button to launch the following DRC dialog:

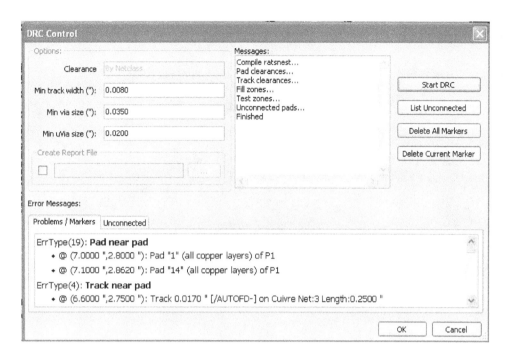

Adjust the parameters accordingly and then press the "Start DRC" button.

This final check will prevent any unpleasant surprises.

11.3 Setting coordinates origin

Set the coordinates origin for the photo plot and drill files, one must place the auxiliary axis on this origin. Activate the icon 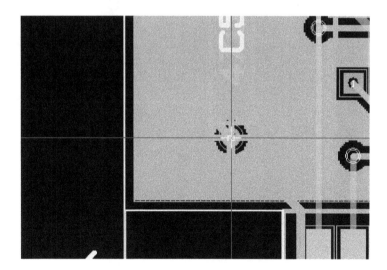. Move the auxiliary axis by left-clicking on the chosen location.

11.4 Generating files for photo-tracing

This is done via the Files/Plot menu option and invokes the following dialog:

Usually, the files are in the GERBER format. Nevertheless, it is possible to produce output in both HPGL and POSTSCRIPT formats. When Postscript format is selected, this dialog will appear.

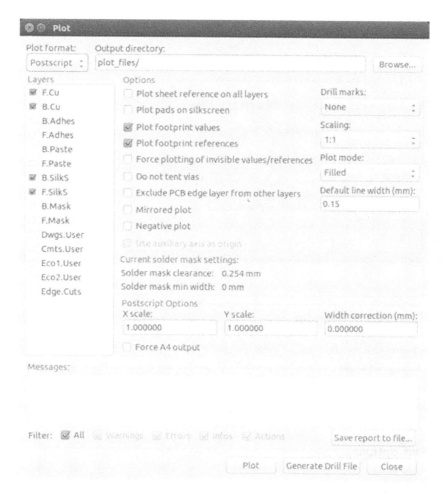

In these formats, a fine scale adjust can be used to compensate for the plotter accuracy and to have a true scale of 1 for the output:

11.4.1 GERBER format

For each layer, Pcbnew generates a separate file following the GERBER 274X standard, by default in 4.6 format (each coordinate in the file is represented by 10 digits, of which 4 are before the decimal point and 6 follow it), units in inches, and a scale of 1.

It is normally necessary to create files for all of the copper layers and, depending on the circuit, for the silkscreen, solder mask, and solder paste layers. All of these files can be produced in one step, by selecting the appropriate check boxes.

For example, for a double-sided circuit with silkscreen, solder mask and solder paste (for SMD components), 8 files should be generated (*xxxx* represents the name of the .brd file).

- xxxx-F_Cu.gbr for the component side.

- xxxx-B_Cu.gbr for the copper side.

- xxxx-F_SilkS.gbr for the component-side silkscreen markings.

- xxxx-B_SilkS.gbr for the copper-side silkscreen markings.

- xxxx-F_Paste.gbr for the component-side solder paste.

- xxxx-B_Paste.gbr for the copper-side solder paste.

- xxxx-F_Mask.gbr for the component-side solder mask.

- xxxx-B_Mask.gbr for the copper-side solder mask.

GERBER file format:

The format used by Pcbnew is RS274X format 4.6, Imperial, Leading zero omitted, Abs format. These are very usual settings.

11.4.2 POSTSCRIPT format

The standard extension for the output files is .ps in the case of postscript output. As for HPGL output, the tracing can be at user-selected scales and can be mirrored. If the Org = Centre option is active, the origin for the coordinates of the tracing table is assumed to be in the centre of the drawing.

If the Print Sheet Ref option is active, the sheet cartridge is traced.

11.4.3 Plot options

Gerber format:

Other formats:

Options

- [ ] Plot sheet reference on all layers
- [ ] Plot pads on silkscreen
- [x] Plot footprint values
- [x] Plot footprint references
- [ ] Force plotting of invisible values/references
- [ ] Do not tent vias
- [ ] Exclude PCB edge layer from other layers
- [ ] Mirrored plot
- [ ] Negative plot
- [ ] Use auxiliary axis as origin

Current solder mask settings:
Solder mask clearance: 0.254 mm
Solder mask min width: 0 mm

Drill marks:
None

Scaling:
1:1

Plot mode:
Filled

Default line width (mm):
0.15

GERBER format specific options:

Use Protel filename extensions	Use .gbl .gtl .gbs .gts .gbp .gtp .gbo .gto instead of .gbr for file name extensions.
Include extended attributes	Output extended attributes to file.
Subtract soldermask from silkscreen	Remove all Silk from solder paste areas.

11.4.4 Other formats

The standard extension depends on the output file type.

Some options are not available for some formats.

The plot can be done at user-selected scales and can be mirrored.

The Print Drill Opt list offers the option of pads that are filled, drilled to the correct diameter or drilled with a small hole (to guide hand drilling).

If the Print Sheet Ref option is active, the sheet cartridge is traced.

11.5 Global clearance settings for the solder stop and the solder paste mask

Mask clearance values can be set globally for the solder mask layers and the solder paste layers. These clearances can be set at the following levels.

- At pads level.

- At footprint level.

- Globally.

And Pcbnew uses by priority order.

- Pad values. If null:

- Footprint values. If null:

- Global values.

11.5.1 Access

The menu option for this is available via the Dimensions menu:

The dialog box is the following:

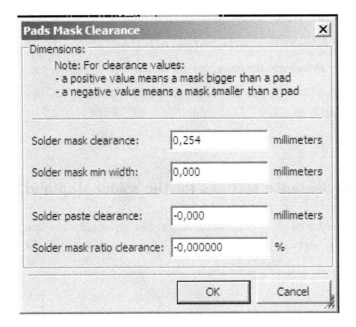

11.5.2 Solder mask clearance

A value near to 0.2 mm is usually good. This value is positive because the mask is usually bigger than the pad.

One can set a minimum value for the solder mask width, between 2 pads.

If the actual value is smaller than the minimum value, the 2 solder mask shapes will be merged.

11.5.3 Solder paste clearance

The final clearance is the sum of the solder paste clearance and a percentage of the pad size.

This value is negative because the mask is usually smaller than the pad.

11.6 Generating drill files

The creation of a drill file xxxx.drl following the EXCELLON standard is always necessary.

One can also produce an optional drill report, and an optional drill map.

- The drill map can be plotted using several formats.
- The drill report is a plain text file.

The generation of these files is controlled via:

- "Create Drill File" button, or
- Files/Fabrication Outputs/Drill file menu selection.

The Drill tools dialog box will be the following:

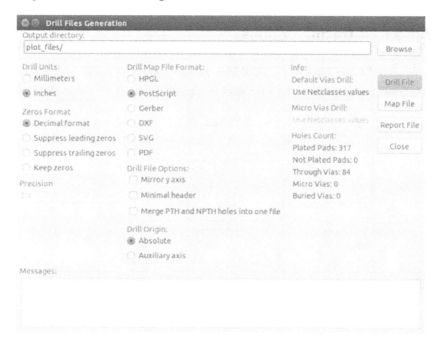

For setting the coordinate origin, the following dialog box is used:

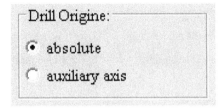

- Absolute: absolute coordinate system is used.

- Auxiliary axis: coordinates are relative to the auxiliary axis, use the icon (right toolbar) to set it.

11.7   Generating wiring documentation

To produce wiring documentation files, the component and copper silkscreen layers can be traced. Usually, just the component-side silkscreen markings are sufficient for wiring a PCB. If the copper-side silkscreen is used, the text it contains should be mirrored in order to be readable.

11.8   Generation of files for automatic component insertion

This option is accessed via the Postprocess/Create Cmp file menu option. However, no file will be generated unless at least one footprint has the Normal+Insert attribute activated (see Editing Footprints). One or two files will be produced, depending upon whether insertable components are present on one or both sides of the PCB. A dialogue box will display the names of the file(s) created.

11.9   Advanced tracing options

The options described below (part of the Files/Plot dialogue) allow for fine-grained control of the tracing process. They are particularly useful when printing the silkscreen markings for wiring documentation.

Options
- [ ] Plot sheet reference on all layers
- [ ] Plot pads on silkscreen
- [x] Plot footprint values
- [x] Plot footprint references
- [ ] Force plotting of invisible values/references
- [ ] Do not tent vias
- [ ] Exclude PCB edge layer from other layers
- [ ] Mirrored plot
- [ ] Negative plot
- [ ] Use auxiliary axis as origin

Current solder mask settings:
Solder mask clearance: 0.254 mm
Solder mask min width: 0 mm

Gerber Options
- [ ] Use Protel filename extensions
- [ ] Include extended attributes
- [ ] Subtract soldermask from silkscreen

Drill marks:
None

Scaling:
1:1

Plot mode:
Filled

Default line width (mm):
0.15

Format
- ( ) 4.5 (unit mm)
- (•) 4.6 (unit mm)

The available options are:

Plot sheet reference on all layers	Trace sheet outline and the cartridge.
Plot pads on silkscreen	Enables/disables printing of pad outlines on the silkscreen layers (if the pads have already been declared to appear on these layers). Prevents any pads from being printed in the disabled mode.
Plot footprint values	Enables printing of VALUE text on the silkscreen.
Plot footprint references	Enables printing of the REFERENCE text on the silkscreen.
Force plotting of invisible values/ references	Forces printing of fields (reference, value) declared as invisible. In combination with *Plot footprint values* and *Plot footprint references*, this option enables production of documents for guiding wiring and repair. These options have proven necessary for circuits using components that are too small (SMD) to allow readable placement of two separate text fields.
Do not tent vias	Delete the mask over the vias.
Exclude PCB edge layer from other layers	GERBER format specific. Do not plot graphic items on edge layer.
Use Protel filename extensions	GERBER format specific. When creating files, use specific extensions for each file. If disabled the Gerber file extension is .gbr.

Chapter 12

Footprint Editor - Managing Libraries

12.1 Overview of Footprint Editor

Pcbnew can simultaneously maintain several libraries. Thus, when a footprint is loaded, all libraries that appear in the library list are searched until the first instance of the footprint is found. In what follows, note that the active library is the library selected within the Footprint Editor, the program will now be described

Footprint Editor enables the creation and the editing of footprints:

- Adding and removing pads.

- Changing pad properties (shape, layer) for individual pads or globally for all pads of a footprint.

- Editing graphic elements (lines, text).

- Editing information fields (value, reference, etc.).

- Editing the associated documentation (description, keywords).

Footprint Editor allows the maintenance of the active library as well by:

- Listing the footprints in the active library.

- Deletion of a footprint from the active library.

- Saving a footprint to the active library.

- Saving all of the footprints contained by a printed circuit.

It is also possible to create new libraries.

The library extension is .mod.

12.2   Accessing Footprint Editor

The Footprint Editor can be accessed in two different ways:

- Directly, via the icon  in the main toolbar of Pcbnew.

- In the edit dialog for the active footprint (see figure below: accessed via the context menu), there is the button Footprint Editor.

In this case, the active footprint of the board will be loaded automatically in Footprint Editor, enabling immediate editing or archiving.

12.3   Footprint Editor user interface

By calling Footprint Editor the following window will appear:

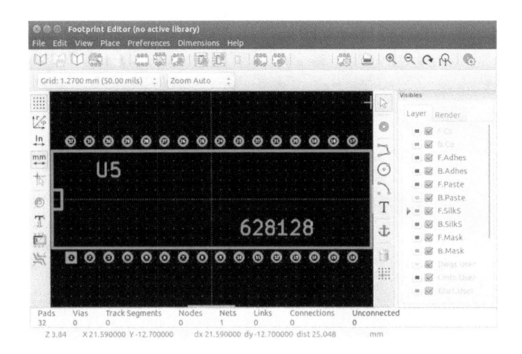

12.4   Top toolbar in Footprint Editor

From this toolbar, the following functions are available:

	Select the active library.
	Save the current footprint to the active library, and write it to disk.
	Create a new library and save the current footprint in it.
	Open the Footprint Viewer
	Access a dialog for deleting a footprint from the active library.
	Create a new footprint.
	Create a footprint using a wizard
	Load a footprint from the active library.
	Load (import) a footprint from the printed circuit board.

	Export the current footprint to the printed circuit board. when the footprint was previously imported from the current board. It will replace the corresponding footprint on the board (i.e., respecting position and orientation).
	Export the current footprint to the printed circuit board. It will be copied on to the printed circuit board at position 0.
	Import a footprint from a file created by the Export command.
	Export a footprint. This command is essentially identical to that for creating a library, the only difference being that it creates a library in the user directory, while creating a library in the standard library directory (usually kicad/modules).
	Undo and Redo
	Invokes the footprint properties dialog.
	Call the print dialog.
	Standard zoom commands.
	Call the pad editor.
	Perform a check of footprint correctness

12.5 Creating a new library

The creation of a new library is done via the button , in this case the file is created by default in the library directory or via the button , in which case the file is created by default in your working directory.

A file-choosing dialog allows the name of the library to be specified and its directory to be changed. In both cases, the library will contain the footprint being edited.

⚠ **Warning**

If an old library of the same name exists, it will be overwritten without warning.

12.6 Saving a footprint in the active library

The action of saving a footprint (thereby modifying the file of the active library) is performed using this button . If a footprint of the same name already exists, it will be replaced. Since you will depend upon the accuracy of the library footprints, it is worth double-checking the footprint before saving.

It is recommended to edit either the reference or value field text to the name of the footprint as identified in the library.

12.7 Transferring a footprint from one library to another

- Select the source library via the button .

- Load the footprint via the button .

- Select the destination library via the button .

- Save the footprint via the button

You may also wish to delete the source footprint.

- Reselect the source library with

- Delete the old footprint via the button 🗑

12.8 Saving all footprints of your board in the active library

It is possible to copy all of the footprints of a given board design to the active library. These footprints will keep their current library names. This command has two uses:

- To create an archive or complete a library with the footprints from a board, in the event of the loss of a library.

- More importantly, it facilitates library maintenance by enabling the production of documentation for the library, as below.

12.9 Documentation for library footprints

It is strongly recommended to document the footprints you create, in order to enable rapid and error-free searching.

For example, who is able to remember all of the multiple pin-out variants of a TO92 package? The Footprint Properties dialog offers a simple solution to this problem.

This dialog accepts:

- A one-line comment/description.
- Multiple keywords.

The description is displayed with the component list in Cvpcb and, in Pcbnew, it is used in the footprint selection dialogs.

The keywords enable searches to be restricted to those footprints corresponding to particular keywords.

When directly loading a footprint (the icon  of the right-hand Pcbnew toolbar), keywords may be entered in the dialog box. Thus, entering the text =CONN will cause the display of the list of footprints whose keyword lists contain the word CONN.

12.10   Documenting libraries - recommended practice

It is recommended to create libraries indirectly, by creating one or more auxiliary circuit boards that constitute the source of (part of) the library, as follows: Create a circuit board in A4 format, in order to be able to print easily to scale (scale = 1).

Create the footprints that the library will contain on this circuit board. The library itself will be created with the File/Archive footprints/Create footprint archive command.

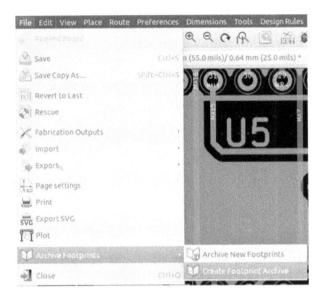

The "true source" of the library will thus be the auxiliary circuit board, and it is on this circuit that any subsequent alterations of footprints will be made. Naturally, several circuit boards can be saved in the same library.

It is generally a good idea to make different libraries for different kinds of components (connectors, discretes,···), since Pcbnew is able to search many libraries when loading footprints.

Here is an example of such a library source:

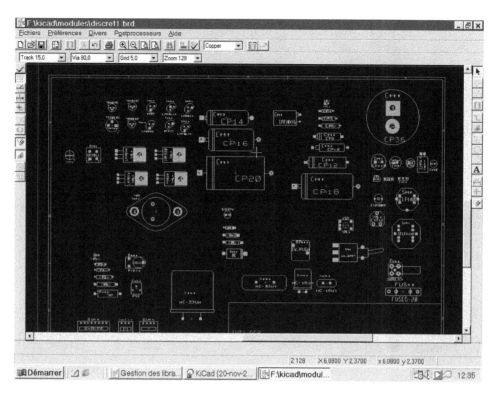

This technique has several advantages:

- The circuit can be printed to scale and serve as documentation for the library with no further effort.

- Future changes of Pcbnew may require regeneration of the libraries, something that can be done very quickly if circuit-board sources of this type have been used. This is important, because the circuit board file formats are guaranteed to remain compatible during future development, but this is not the case for the library file format.

12.11   Footprint Libraries Management

The list of footprint libraries in Pcbnew can be edited using the Footprint Libraries Manager. This allows you to add and remove footprint libraries by hand, and also allows you to invoke the Footprint Libraries Wizard by pressing the "Append With Wizard" button.

The Footprint Libraries Wizard can also be invoked through the Preferences menu, and can automatically add a library (detecting its type) from a file or from a Github URL. The URL for the official libraries is: https://github.com/KiCad

More details about footprint library tables and the Manager and Wizard can be found in the CvPcb Reference Manual in the section *Footprint Library Tables*.

12.12   3D Shapes Libraries Management

The 3D shape libraries can be downloaded by 3D Shape Libraries Wizard. It can be invoked from the menu Preferences → 3D Shapes Libraries Downloader.

Chapter 13

Footprint Editor - Creating and Editing Footprints

13.1 Footprint Editor overview

Footprint Editor is used for editing and creating PCB footprints. This includes:

- Adding and removing pads.

- Changing pad properties (shape, layer), for individual pads or for all the pads in a footprint.

- Adding and editing graphic elements (contours, text).

- Editing fields (value, reference, etc.).

- Editing the associated documentation (description, keywords).

13.2 Footprint elements

A footprint is the physical representation (footprint) of the part to be inserted in the PCB and it must be linked to the relative component in your schematic. Each footprint includes three different elements:

- The pads.

- Graphical contours and text.

- Fields.

In addition, a number of other parameters must be correctly defined if the auto-placement function will be used. The same holds for the generation of auto-insertion files.

13.2.1 Pads

Two pad properties are important:

- Geometry (shape, layers, drill holes).

- The pad number, which is constituted by up to four alphanumeric characters. Thus, the following are all valid pad numbers: 1, 45 and 9999, but also AA56 and ANOD. The pad number must be identical to that of the corresponding pin number in the schematic, because it defines the matching pin and pad numbers that Pcbnew links pins and pads with.

13.2.2 Contours

Graphical contours are used to draw the physical shape of the footprint. Several different types of contour are available: lines, circles, arcs, and text. Contours have no electrical significance, they are simply graphical aids.

13.2.3 Fields

These are text elements associated with a footprint. Two are obligatory and always present: the reference field and the value field. These are automatically read and updated by Pcbnew when a netlist is read during the loading of footprints into your board. The reference is replaced by the appropriate schematic reference (U1, IC3, etc.). The value is replaced by the value of the corresponding part in the schematic (47K, 74LS02, etc.). Other fields can be added and these will behave like graphical text.

13.3 Starting Footprint Editor and selecting a footprint to edit

Footprint Editor can be started in two ways:

- Directly via the icon from the main toolbar of Pcbnew. This allows the creation or modification of a footprint in the library.

- Double-clicking a footprint will launch the *Footprint Properties* menu, which offers a *Go to Footprint Editor* button. If this option is used, the footprint from the board will be loaded into the editor, for modification or for saving.

13.4 Footprint Editor Toolbars

Calling Footprint Editor will launch a new window that looks like this:

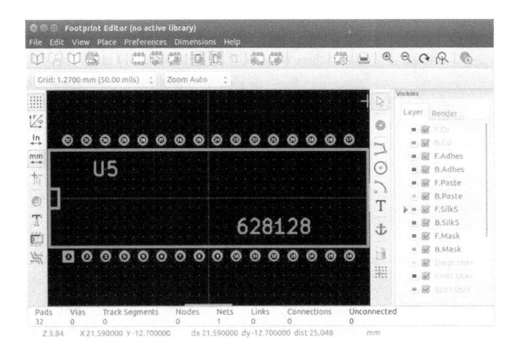

13.4.1 Edit toolbar (right-hand side)

This toolbar contains tools for:

- Placing pads.

- Adding graphic elements (contours, text).

- Positioning the anchor.

- Deleting elements.

The specific functions are the following:

⬚	No tool.
◉	Add pads.
⌐◦⌐	Draw line segments and polygons.
◎	Draw circles.
⌒	Draw circular arcs.
T	Add graphical text (fields are not managed by this tool).
⚓	Position the footprint anchor.

	Delete elements.
	Grid origin. (grid offset). Useful for placement of pads. The grid origin can be put on a given location (the first pad to place), and after the grid size can be set to the pad pitch. Placing pads is therefore very easy

13.4.2   Display toolbar (left-hand side)

These tools manage the display options in Footprint Editor:

	Display the grid.
	Display polar coordinates.
mm In	Use units of mm or inch
	Toggle cursor crosshair shape
	Display pad in outline mode.
	Display text in outline mode.
	Display contours in outline mode.
	Toggle high-contrast mode

13.5   Context Menus

The right mouse button calls up menus that depend upon the element beneath the cursor.

The context menu for editing footprint parameters:

The context menu for editing pads:

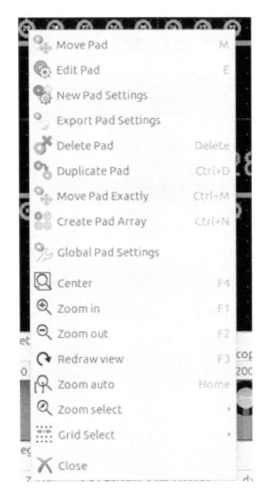

The context menu for editing graphic elements:

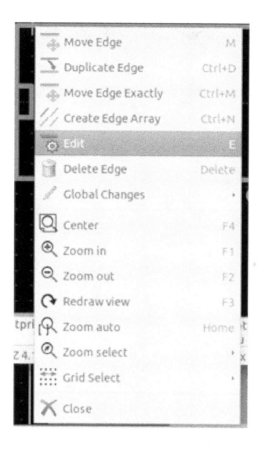

13.6 Footprint properties dialog

This dialog can be launched when the cursor is over a footprint by clicking on the right mouse button and then selecting *Edit Footprint*.

The dialog can be used to define the main footprint parameters.

13.7 Creating a new footprint

A new footprint can be created via the button . The name of the new footprint will be requested. This will be the name by which the footprint will be identified in the library.

This text also serves as the footprint value, which is ultimately replaced by the real value (100 μF_16 V, 100 Ω_0.5 W, ⋯).

The new footprint will require:

- Contours (and possibly graphic text).

- Pads.

- A value (hidden text that is replaced by the true value when used).

Alternative method:

When a new footprint is similar to an existing footprint in a library or a circuit board, an alternative and quicker method of creating the new footprint is as follows:

- Load the similar footprint ( , or).

- Modify the "Footprint Name in Library" field in order to generate a new identifier (name).

- Edit and save the new footprint.

13.8 Adding and editing pads

Once a footprint has been created, pads can be added, deleted or modified. Modification of pads can be local, affecting only the pad under the cursor, or global, affecting all pads of the footprint.

13.8.1 Adding pads

Select the   icon from the right hand toolbar. Pads can be added by clicking in the desired position with the left mouse button. Pad properties are predefined in the pad properties menu.

Do not forget to enter the pad number.

13.8.2 Setting pad properties

This can be done in three different ways:

- Selecting the   icon from the horizontal toolbar.

- Clicking on an existing pad and selecting *Edit Pad*. The pad' s settings can then be edited.

- Clicking on an existing pad and selecting *Export Pad Settings*. In this case, the geometrical properties of the selected pad will become the default pad properties.

In the first two cases, the following dialog window will be displayed:

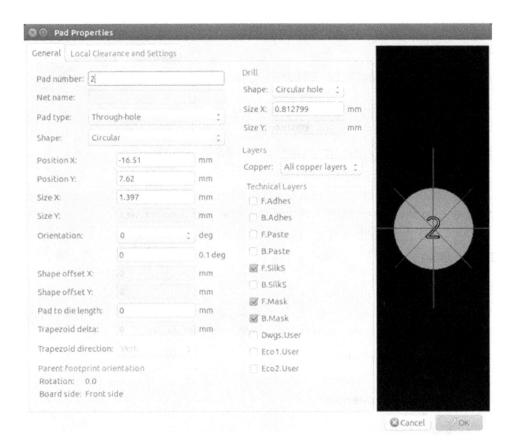

Care should be taken to define correctly the layers to which the pad will belong. In particular, although copper layers are easy to define, the management of non-copper layers (solder mask, solder pads···) is equally important for circuit manufacture and documentation.

The Pad Type selector triggers an automatic selection of layers that is generally sufficient.

13.8.2.1 Rectangular pads

For SMD footprints of the VQFP/PQFP type which have rectangular pads on all four sides (both horizontal and vertical) it is recommended to use just one shape (for example, a horizontal rectangle) and to place it with different orientations (0 for horizontal and 90 degrees for vertical). Global resizing of pads can then be done in a single operation.

13.8.2.2 Rotate pads

Rotations of -90 or -180 are only required for trapezoidal pads used in microwave footprints.

13.8.2.3 Non-plated through hole pads

Pads can be defined as Non-Plated Through Hole pads (NPTH pads).

These pads must be defined on one or all copper layers (obviously, the hole exists on all copper layers).

This requirement allows you to define specific clearance parameters (for instance clearance for a screw).

When the pad hole size is the same as the pad size, for a round or oval pad, this pad is NOT plotted on copper layers in GERBER files.

These pads are used for mechanical purposes, therefore no pad name or net name is allowed. A connection to a net is not possible.

13.8.2.4 Pads not on copper layers

These are unusual pads. This option can be used to create fiducials or masks on technical layers.

13.8.2.5 Offset parameter

Pad 3 has an offset Y = 15 mils:

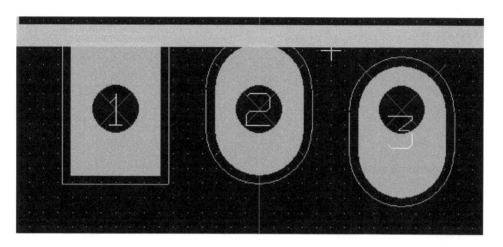

13.8.2.6 Delta Parameter (trapezoidal pads)

Pad 1 has its parameter Delta X = 10 mils

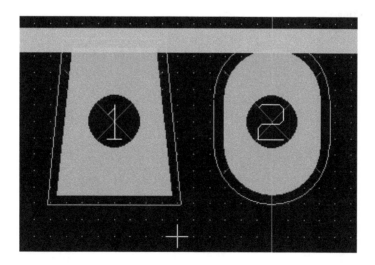

13.8.3   Setting clearance for solder mask and solder paste mask layers

Setting a clearance can be made at 3 levels:

- Global level.

- Footprint level.

- Pad level.

Pcbnew uses the following to calculate clearances:

- Pad settings. If null,

- Footprint settings. If null,

- Global settings.

13.8.3.1   Remarks

The solder mask pad shape is usually bigger than the pad itself. So the clearance value is positive. The solder paste mask pad shape is usually smaller than the pad itself. So the clearance value is negative.

13.8.3.2   Solder paste mask parameters

For solder paste mask there are two parameters:

- A fixed value.

- A percentage of the pad size.

The real value is the sum of these two values.

Footprint level settings:

Pad level settings:

13.9 Fields Properties

There are at least two fields: reference and value.

Their parameters (attribute, size, width) must be updated. You can access the dialog box from the pop-up menu, by double clicking on the field, or by the footprint properties dialog box:

13.10 Automatic placement of a footprint

If the user wishes to exploit the full capabilities of the auto-placement functions, it is necessary to define the allowed orientations of the footprint (Footprint Properties dialog).

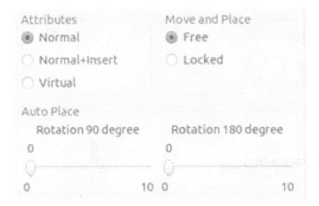

Usually, rotation of 180 degrees is permitted for resistors, non-polarized capacitors and other symmetrical elements.

Some footprints (small transistors, for example) are often permitted to rotate by +/- 90 or 180 degrees. By default, a new footprint will have its rotation permissions set to zero. This can be adjusted according to the following rule:

A value of 0 makes rotation impossible, 10 allows it completely, and any intermediate value represents a limited rotation. For example, a resistor might have a permission of 10 to rotate 180 degrees (unrestrained) and a permission of 5 for a +/- 90 degree rotation (allowed, but discouraged).

13.11 Attributes

The attributes window is the following:

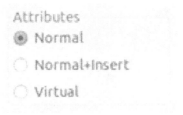

- Normal is the standard attribute.

- Normal+Insert indicates that the footprint must appear in the automatic insertion file (for automatic insertion machines). This attribute is most useful for surface mount components (SMDs).

- Virtual indicates that a component is directly formed by the circuit board. Examples would be edge connectors or inductors created by a particular track shape (as sometimes seen in microwave footprints).

13.12 Documenting footprints in a library

It is strongly recommended to document newly created footprints, in order to facilitate their rapid and accurate retrieval. Who is able to recall the multiple pin-out variants of a TO92 footprint?

The Footprint Properties dialog offers a simple and yet powerful means for documentation generation.

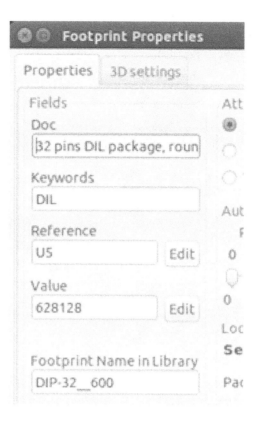

This menu allows:

- The entry of a comment line (description).

- Multiple keywords.

The comment line is displayed with the component list in CvPcb and in the footprint selection menus in Pcbnew. The keywords can be used to restrict searches to those parts possessing the given keywords.

Thus, while using the load footprint command (icon in the right-hand toolbar in Pcbnew), it is possible to type the text =TO220 into the dialog box to have Pcbnew display a list of the footprints possessing the keyword TO220

13.13   3-dimensional visualisation

A footprint may have been associated with a file containing a three-dimensional representation of itself. In order to associate such a file with a footprint, select the 3D Settings tab. The options panel is the following:

The data information should be provided:

- The file containing the 3D representation (created by the 3D modeler Wings3D, in vrml format, via the export to vrml command).

- The default path is kicad/modules/package3d. In the example, the file name is discret/to_220horiz.wrl, using the default path)

- The x, y and z scales.

- The offset with respect to the anchor point of the footprint (usually zero).

- The initial rotation in degrees about each axis (usually zero).

Setting scale allows:

- To use the same 3D file for footprints which have similar shapes but different sizes (resistors, capacitors, SMD components···)

- For small (or very large) packages, a better use of the Wings3D grid is to scale **0.1 inch in Pcbnew = 1 grid unit** in Wings3D.

If such a file has been specified, it is possible to view the component in 3D.

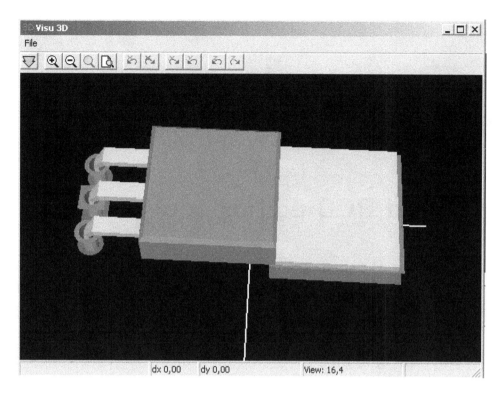

The 3D model will automatically appear in the 3D representation of the printed circuit board.

13.14 Saving a footprint into the active library

The save command (modification of the file of the active library) is activated by the button.

If a footprint of the same name exists (an older version), it will be overwritten. Because it is important to be able to have confidence in the library footprints, it is worth double-checking the footprint for errors before saving.

Before saving, it is also recommended to change the reference or value of the footprint to be equal to the library name of the footprint.

13.15 Saving a footprint to the board

If the edited footprint comes from the current board, the button will update this footprint on the board.

Chapter 14

Advanced PCB editing tools

There are some more advanced editing tools available in Pcbnew and Footprint Editor, which can help you to efficiently lay out components on the canvas.

14.1 Duplicating items

Duplication is a method to clone an item and pick it up in the same action. It is broadly similar to copy-and-pasting, but it allows you to "sprinkle" components over the PCB and it allows you to manually lay out components using the "Move Exact" tool (see below) more easily.

Duplication is done by using the hotkey (which defaults to Ctrl-D) or the duplicate item option in the context menu. In the legacy renderer, these appear as below, depending on the item type:

14.2 Moving items exactly

The "Move Exact" tool allows you to move an item (or group of items) by a certain amount, which can be entered in Cartesian or polar formats and which can be entered in any supported units. This is useful when it would otherwise be cumbersome to switch to a different grid, or when a feature is not spaced according to any existing grids.

To use this tool, select the items you wish to move and then use either the hotkey (defaults to Ctrl-M) or the context menu items to invoke the dialog. You can also invoke the dialog with the hotkey when moving or duplicating items, which can make it easy to repeatedly apply an offset to multiple components.

Move exact with Cartesian move vector entry

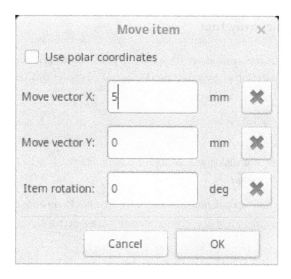

Move exact with polar move vector entry

The checkbox allows you to switch between Cartesian and polar co-ordinate systems. Whatever is currently in the form will be converted automatically to the other system.

Then you enter the desired move vector. You can use the units indicated by the labels ("mm" in the images above) or you can specify the units yourself (e.g. "1 in" for an inch, or "2 rad" for 2 radians).

Pressing OK will apply the translation to the selection, and cancel will close the dialog and the items will not be moved. If OK is pressed, the move vector will be saved and pre-filled next time the dialog is opened, which allows repeated application of the same vector to multiple objects.

14.3 Array tools

Pcbnew and the Footprint Editor both have assistants for creating arrays of features and components, which can be used to easily and accurately lay out repetitive elements on PCBs and in footprints.

14.3.1 Activating the array tool

The array tool acts on the component under the cursor, or, in GAL mode, on a selection. It can be accessed either via the context menu for the selection or by a keyboard shortcut (defaults to Ctrl-N). In legacy mode, the context menu icons indicate an array of the selected type:

The array tool is presented as a dialog window, with a pane for the types of arrays. There are two types of arrays supported so far: grid, and circular.

Each type of array can be fully specified on the respective panes. Geometric options (how the grid is laid out) go on the left; numbering options (including how the numbers progress across the grid) on the right.

14.3.2 Grid arrays

Grid arrays are arrays that lay components out according to a 2-dimensional square grid. This kind of array can also produce a linear array by only laying out a single row or column.

The settings dialog for grid arrays look like this:

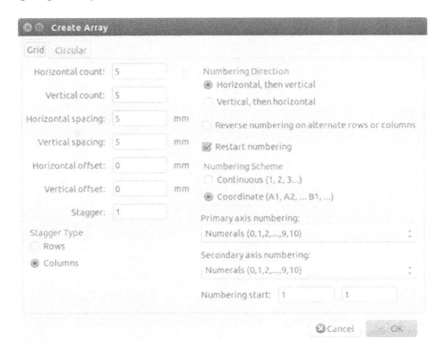

14.3.2.1 Geometric options

The geometric options are as follow:

- **Horrizontal count**: the number of "columns" in the grid.

- **Vertical count**: the number of "rows" in the grid.

- **Horizontal spacing**: the horizontal distance from item to the item in the same row and next column. If this is negative, the grid progresses from right to left.

- **Vertical spacing**: the vertical distance from one item to the item in the same column and the next row. If this is negative, the grid progress bottom to top.

- **Horizontal offset**: start each row this distance to the right of the previous one

- **Vertical offset**: start each column this distance below the previous one

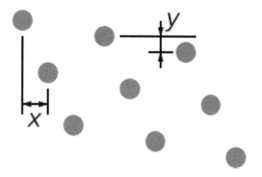

Figure 14.1: 3x3 grid with x and y offsets

- **Stagger**: add an offset to every set of "n" rows/columns, with each row progressing by $1/n'$ th of the relevant spacing dimension:

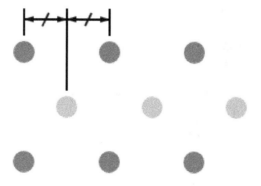

Figure 14.2: 3x3 grid with a row stagger of 2

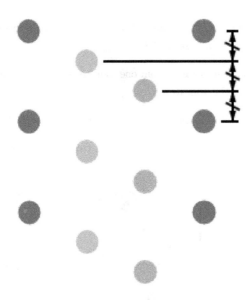

Figure 14.3: 4x3 grid with a column stagger of 3

14.3.2.2 Numbering options

- **Numbering Direction**: Determines whether numbers proceed along rows and then moves to the next row, or down columns and then to the next column. Note that the direction on numbering is defined by the sign of the spacing: a negative spacing will result in right-to-left or bottom-to-top numbering.

- **Reverse numbering on alternate rows or columns**: If selected, the numbering order (left-to-right or right-to-left, for example) on alternate rows or columns. Whether rows or columns alternate depends on the numbering direction. This option is useful for packages like DIPs where the numbering proceeds up one side and down the other.

- **Restart numbering**: if laying out using items that already have numbers, reset to the start, otherwise continue if possible from this item's number

- **Numbering Scheme**

  - **Continuous**: the numbering just continues across a row/column break - if the last item in the first row is numbered "7", the first item in the second row will be "8".

  - **Coordinate**: the numbering uses a two-axis scheme where the number is made up of the row and column index. Which one comes first (row or column) is determined by the numbering direction.

- **Axis numberings**: what "alphabet" to use to number the axes. Choices are

  - **Numerals** for normal integer indices

  - **Hexadecimal** for base-16 indexing

  - **Alphabetic, minus IOSQXZ**, a common scheme for electronic components, recommended by ASME Y14.35M-1997 sec. 5.2 (previously MIL-STD-100 sec. 406.5) to avoid confusion with numerals.

  - **Full alphabet** from A-Z.

14.3.3 Circular arrays

Circular arrays lay out items around a circle or a circular arc. The circle is defined by the location of the selection (or the centre of a selected group) and a centre point that is specified. Below is the circular array configuration dialog:

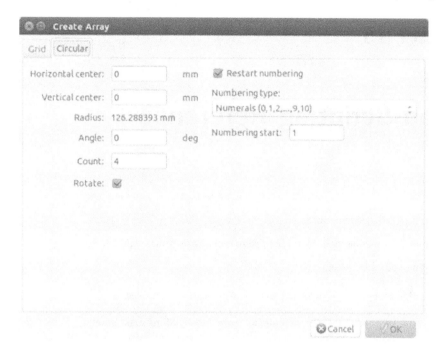

14.3.3.1 Geometric options

- **Horizontal center, Vertical center**: The centre of the circle. The radius field below will update automatically when you adjust these.

- **Angle**: The angular difference between two adjacent items in the array. Set this to zero to evenly divide the circle with "count" elements.

- **Count**: Number of items in the array (including the original item)

- **Rotate**: Rotate each item around its own location. Otherwise, the item will be translated but not rotated (for example, a square pad will always remain upright if this option is not set).

14.3.3.2 Numbering options

Circular arrays have only one dimension and a simpler geometry than grids. The meanings of the available options are the same as for grids. Items are numbered clockwise - for an anticlockwise array, specify a negative angle.

Chapter 15

KiCad Scripting Reference

Scripting allows you to automate tasks within KiCad using the Python language.

Also see the doxygen documentation on Python Scripting Reference.

You can see python module help by typing `pydoc pcbnew` on your terminal.

Using scripting you can create:

- **Plugins**: this type of script is loaded when KiCad starts. Examples:

  - **Footprint Wizards**: To help you build footprints easily filling in parameters. See the dedicated section Footprint Wizards below.

  - **File I/O** *(planned)*: To let you write plugins to export/import other filetypes

  - **Actions** *(planned)*: Associate events to scripting actions or register new menus or toolbar icons.

- **Command Line Scripts**: scripts that can be used from the command line, load boards or libraries, modify them, and render outputs or new boards.

It shall be noted that the only KiCad applicaiton that supports scripting is Pcbnew. It is also planned for Eeschema in the future.

15.1 KiCad Objects

The scripting API reflects the internal object structure inside KiCad/pcbnew. BOARD is the main object, that has a set of properties and a set of MODULEs, and TRACKs/VIAs, TEXTE_PCB, DIMENSION, DRAWSEGMENT. Then MODULEs have D_PADs, EDGEs, etc.

- See the BOARD section below.

15.2 Basic API Reference

All the pcbnew API is provided from the "pcbnew" module in Python. GetBoard() method will return the current pcb open at editor, useful for commands written from the integrated scripting shell inside pcbnew or action plugins.

15.3   Loading and Saving a Board

- **LoadBoard(filename):** loads a board from file returning a BOARD object, using the file format that matches the filename extension.

- **SaveBoard(filename,board):** saves a BOARD object to file, using the file format that matches the filename extension.

- **board.Save(filename):** same as above, but it's a method of BOARD object.

Example that loads a board, hides all values, shows all references

```
#!/usr/bin/env python2.7
import sys
from pcbnew import *


filename=sys.argv[1]


pcb = LoadBoard(filename)
for module in pcb.GetModules():
    print "* Module: %s"%module.GetReference()
    module.Value().SetVisible(False)        # set Value as Hidden
    module.Reference().SetVisible(True)      # set Reference as Visible


pcb.Save("mod_"+filename)
```

15.4   Listing and Loading Libraries

Enumerate library, enumerate modules, enumerate pads

```
#!/usr/bin/python


from pcbnew import *


libpath = "/usr/share/kicad/modules/Sockets.pretty"
print ">> enumerate footprints, pads of",libpath


# Load the suitable plugin to read/write the .pretty library
# (containing the .kicad_mod footprint files)
src_type = IO_MGR.GuessPluginTypeFromLibPath( libpath );
# Rem: we can force the plugin type by using IO_MGR.PluginFind( IO_MGR.KICAD )
plugin = IO_MGR.PluginFind( src_type )


# Print plugin type name: (Expecting "KiCad" for a .pretty library)
print( "Selected plugin type: %s" % plugin.PluginName() )


list_of_footprints = plugin.FootprintEnumerate(libpath)
```

```
for name in list_of_footprints:
    fp = plugin.FootprintLoad(libpath,name)
    # print the short name of the footprint
    print name  # this is the name inside the loaded library
    # followed by ref field, value field, and decription string:
    # Remember ref and value texts are dummy texts, replaced by the schematic values
    # when reading a netlist.
    print "  ->", fp.GetReference(), fp.GetValue(), fp.GetDescription()

    # print pad info: GetPos0() is the pad position relative to the footrint position
    for pad in fp.Pads():
        print "    pad [%s]" % pad.GetPadName(), "at",\
            "pos0", ToMM(pad.GetPos0().x), ToMM(pad.GetPos0().y),"mm",\
            "shape offset", ToMM(pad.GetOffset().x), ToMM(pad.GetOffset().y), "mm"
    print ""
```

15.5 BOARD

Board is the basic object in KiCad pcbnew, it's the document.

BOARD contains a set of object lists that can be accessed using the following methods, they will return iterable lists that can be iterated using "for obj in list:"

- **board.GetModules():** This method returns a list of MODULE objects, all the modules available in the board will be exposed here.

- **board.GetDrawings():** Returns the list of BOARD_ITEMS that belong to the board drawings

- **board.GetTracks():** This method returns a list of TRACKs and VIAs inside a BOARD

- **board.GetFullRatsnest():** Returns the list of ratsnest (connections still not routed)

- **board.GetNetClasses():** Returns the list of net classes

- **board.GetCurrentNetClassName():** Returns the current net class

- **board.GetViasDimensionsList():** Returns the list of Via dimensions available to the board.

- **board.GetTrackWidthList():** Returns the list of Track Widths available to the board.

Board Inspection Example

```
#!/usr/bin/env python
import sys
from pcbnew import *

filename=sys.argv[1]
```

```
pcb = LoadBoard(filename)

ToUnits = ToMM
FromUnits = FromMM
#ToUnits=ToMils
#FromUnits=FromMils

print "LISTING VIAS:"

for item in pcb.GetTracks():
    if type(item) is VIA:

        pos = item.GetPosition()
        drill = item.GetDrillValue()
        width = item.GetWidth()
        print " * Via:    %s - %f/%f "%(ToUnits(pos),ToUnits(drill),ToUnits(width))

    elif type(item) is TRACK:

        start = item.GetStart()
        end = item.GetEnd()
        width = item.GetWidth()

        print " * Track: %s to %s, width %f" % (ToUnits(start),ToUnits(end),ToUnits(width))

    else:
        print "Unknown type    %s" % type(item)

print ""
print "LIST DRAWINGS:"

for item in pcb.GetDrawings():
    if type(item) is TEXTE_PCB:
        print "* Text:    '%s' at %s"%(item.GetText(), item.GetPosition())
    elif type(item) is DRAWSEGMENT:
        print "* Drawing: %s"%item.GetShapeStr() # dir(item)
    else:
        print type(item)

print ""
print "LIST MODULES:"

for module in pcb.GetModules():
    print "* Module: %s at %s"%(module.GetReference(),ToUnits(module.GetPosition()))

print ""
print "Ratsnest cnt:",len(pcb.GetFullRatsnest())
print "track w cnt:",len(pcb.GetTrackWidthList())
```

```
print "via s cnt:",len(pcb.GetViasDimensionsList())

print ""
print "LIST ZONES:", pcb.GetAreaCount()

for idx in range(0, pcb.GetAreaCount()):
    zone=pcb.GetArea(idx)
    print "zone:", idx, "priority:", zone.GetPriority(), "netname", zone.GetNetname()

print ""
print "NetClasses:", pcb.GetNetClasses().GetCount(),
```

15.6 Examples

15.6.1 Change a component pin's paste mask margin

We only want to change pins from 1 to 14, 15 is a thermal pad that must be kept as it is.

```
#!/usr/bin/env python2.7
import sys
from pcbnew import *

filename=sys.argv[1]
pcb = LoadBoard(filename)

# Find module U304
u304 = pcb.FindModuleByReference('U304')
pads = u304.Pads()

#  Iterate over pads, printing solder paste margin
for p in pads:
    print p.GetPadName(), ToMM(p.GetLocalSolderPasteMargin())
    id = int(p.GetPadName())
    # Set margin to 0 for all but pad (pin) 15
    if id<15: p.SetLocalSolderPasteMargin(0)

pcb.Save("mod_"+filename)
```

15.7 Footprint Wizards

The footprint wizards are a collection of python scripts that can be accessed from the Footprint Editor. If you invoke the footprint dialog you select a given wizard that allows you to see the footprint rendered, and you have some parameters you can edit.

If the plugins are not properly distributed to your system package, you can find the latest versions in the KiCad source tree at launchpad.

They should be located in for example `C:\Program Files\KiCad\share\kicad\scripting\plugins`.

On linux you can also keep your user plugins in `$HOME/.kicad_plugins`.

Build footprints easily filling in parameters.

```python
from __future__ import division
import pcbnew

import HelpfulFootprintWizardPlugin as HFPW


class FPC_FootprintWizard(HFPW.HelpfulFootprintWizardPlugin):

    def GetName(self):
        return "FPC (SMT connector)"

    def GetDescription(self):
        return "FPC (SMT connector) Footprint Wizard"

    def GetValue(self):
        pins = self.parameters["Pads"]["*n"]
        return "FPC_%d" % pins

    def GenerateParameterList(self):
        self.AddParam( "Pads", "n", self.uNatural, 40 )
        self.AddParam( "Pads", "pitch", self.uMM, 0.5 )
        self.AddParam( "Pads", "width", self.uMM, 0.25 )
        self.AddParam( "Pads", "height", self.uMM, 1.6)
        self.AddParam( "Shield", "shield_to_pad", self.uMM, 1.6 )
        self.AddParam( "Shield", "from_top", self.uMM, 1.3 )
        self.AddParam( "Shield", "width", self.uMM, 1.5 )
        self.AddParam( "Shield", "height", self.uMM, 2 )


    # build a rectangular pad
    def smdRectPad(self,module,size,pos,name):
        pad = pcbnew.D_PAD(module)
        pad.SetSize(size)
        pad.SetShape(pcbnew.PAD_SHAPE_RECT)
        pad.SetAttribute(pcbnew.PAD_ATTRIB_SMD)
        pad.SetLayerSet( pad.SMDMask() )
        pad.SetPos0(pos)
        pad.SetPosition(pos)
        pad.SetPadName(name)
        return pad
```

```
def CheckParameters(self):
    p = self.parameters
    self.CheckParamInt( "Pads", "*n" )   # not internal units preceded by "*"



def BuildThisFootprint(self):
    p = self.parameters
    pad_count       = int(p["Pads"]["*n"])
    pad_width       = p["Pads"]["width"]
    pad_height      = p["Pads"]["height"]
    pad_pitch       = p["Pads"]["pitch"]
    shl_width       = p["Shield"]["width"]
    shl_height      = p["Shield"]["height"]
    shl_to_pad      = p["Shield"]["shield_to_pad"]
    shl_from_top    = p["Shield"]["from_top"]

    offsetX         = pad_pitch * ( pad_count-1 ) / 2
    size_pad = pcbnew.wxSize( pad_width, pad_height )
    size_shld = pcbnew.wxSize(shl_width, shl_height)
    size_text = self.GetTextSize()   # IPC nominal

    # Gives a position and size to ref and value texts:
    textposy = pad_height/2 + pcbnew.FromMM(1) + self.GetTextThickness()
    self.draw.Reference( 0, textposy, size_text )

    textposy = textposy + size_text + self.GetTextThickness()
    self.draw.Value( 0, textposy, size_text )

    # create a pad array and add it to the module
    for n in range ( 0, pad_count ):
        xpos = pad_pitch*n - offsetX
        pad = self.smdRectPad(self.module,size_pad, pcbnew.wxPoint(xpos,0),str(n+1))
        self.module.Add(pad)



    # Mechanical shield pads: left pad and right pad
    xpos = -shl_to_pad-offsetX
    pad_s0_pos = pcbnew.wxPoint(xpos,shl_from_top)
    pad_s0 = self.smdRectPad(self.module, size_shld, pad_s0_pos, "0")
    xpos = (pad_count-1) * pad_pitch+shl_to_pad - offsetX
    pad_s1_pos = pcbnew.wxPoint(xpos,shl_from_top)
    pad_s1 = self.smdRectPad(self.module, size_shld, pad_s1_pos, "0")

    self.module.Add(pad_s0)
    self.module.Add(pad_s1)

    # add footprint outline
    linewidth = self.draw.GetLineTickness()
```

```
margin = linewidth

# upper line
posy = -pad_height/2 - linewidth/2 - margin
xstart = - pad_pitch*0.5-offsetX
xend = pad_pitch * pad_count + xstart;
self.draw.Line( xstart, posy, xend, posy )

# lower line
posy = pad_height/2 + linewidth/2 + margin
self.draw.Line(xstart, posy, xend, posy)

# around left mechanical pad (the outline around right pad is mirrored/y axix)
yend = pad_s0_pos.y + shl_height/2 + margin
self.draw.Line(xstart, posy, xstart, yend)
self.draw.Line(-xstart, posy, -xstart, yend)

posy = yend
xend = pad_s0_pos.x - (shl_width/2 + linewidth + margin*2)
self.draw.Line(xstart, posy, xend, posy)

# right pad side
self.draw.Line(-xstart, posy, -xend, yend)

# vertical segment at left of the pad
xstart = xend
yend = posy - (shl_height + linewidth + margin*2)
self.draw.Line(xstart, posy, xend, yend)

# right pad side
self.draw.Line(-xstart, posy, -xend, yend)

# horizontal segment above the pad
xstart = xend
xend = - pad_pitch*0.5-offsetX
posy = yend
self.draw.Line(xstart, posy, xend, yend)

# right pad side
self.draw.Line(-xstart, posy,-xend, yend)

# vertical segment above the pad
xstart = xend
yend = -pad_height/2 - linewidth/2 - margin
self.draw.Line(xstart, posy, xend, yend)

# right pad side
self.draw.Line(-xstart, posy, -xend, yend)
```

```
FPC_FootprintWizard().register()
```

www.ingramcontent.com/pod-product-compliance
Lightning Source LLC
Chambersburg PA
CBHW082119070326
40690CB00049B/3992